THE
COLOR
OF
SUCCESS

THE
COLOR
OF
SUCCESS

Why Color Matters in

your Life

your Love

your Lexus

By

Mary Ellen Lapp

LIFESUCCESS PUBLISHING, LLC
8900 E Pinnacle Peak Road, Suite D240
Scottsdale, AZ 85255

Telephone:	800.473.7134
Fax:	480.661.1014
E-mail:	admin@lifesuccesspublishing.com
ISBN:	978-1-59930-078-8
Cover:	Lloyd Arbour & LifeSuccess Publishing
Layout:	Lloyd Arbour & LifeSuccess Publishing

COMPANIES, ORGANIZATIONS, INSTITUTIONS, AND INDUSTRY PUBLICATIONS: Quantity discounts are available on bulk purchases of this book for reselling, educational purposes, subscription incentives, gifts, sponsorship, or fundraising. Special books or book excerpts can also be created to fit specific needs such as private labeling with your logo on the cover and a message from a VIP printed inside. For more information please contact our Special Sales Department at LifeSuccess Publishing.

This publication is designed to provide accurate and authoritative information in regard to the subject matter covered. It is sold with the understanding that neither the author nor the publisher is engaged in rendering legal, accounting, or other professional service. If legal advise or other expert assistance is required, the services of a competent professional person should be sought.

CONTENTS

DEDICATION

Courage
Determination

The personification of these hallmarks of success,
I witnessed early in my life.
To my inspiration, my mother, Mary.

Five dollars of your book purchase is donated to
Breast Cancer Research

ACKNOWLEDGEMENTS

Thank you to my family for your encouragement, guidance and loving reminder, "the apple doesn't fall far from the tree." My appreciation goes to the teachers who inspired my love of color and passion for the written word.

I honor the life teachers that showed me how to be all I am meant to be, Jack Canfield, Jim Rohn, and especially Bob Proctor for contributing the foreword of my book.

Thanks to my friends and colleagues for taking care of business while I was otherwise occupied. And thanks to my mastermind group for keeping me accountable to my dreams.

For your patience and belief in me during my single minded obsession, thanks to the love of my life, Keith.

FOREWORD

The power of everyday things to influence us has always fascinated me. Entire industries flourish by making pronouncements about what to wear, where to travel, and what new gadget we must own. The media's prime purpose has become to tell us what to believe about every issue. Our human nature is to be aware of our surroundings and to process the information we observe. Unlike the animal kingdom that responds by instinct to outside stimuli, the gift of being human gives us the opportunity to be not only aware, but to create conditions and environments that serve us. If we choose.

Having this God given ability to create is no guarantee that we always use it. Instead of being master of our surroundings, the majority of people allow outside influences to direct their lives and dictate their surroundings. Without conscious thought, they follow the crowd, mimic their actions and get the results of those around them. Why do you think the people you pass on the street look so alike?

There are subdivisions populated with look-alike houses, freeways full of look-alike cars. And most people complain about coping with the same problems.

If the idea of actively creating your results is new to you, pay close attention to the information in this book. The Color of Success will show you that making your own best choices is the first step in celebrating your uniqueness and creating your personal success. It has been said that our talents and uniqueness are our gifts from God. What we do with those unique talents is our gift to God.

Once you realize the power that color has to create a positive environment for you, you will eagerly make choices that set you apart from the crowd and optimize your results. As Napoleon Hill said, "let me remind you, not to go searching for opportunity in the distance, but reach out and embrace it right where you are." Your best opportunity for success starts with you.

– Bob Proctor
Best Selling author of *You Were Born Rich*

TESTIMONIALS

"Your choices of colors in every area of your business and personal life can have a major impact on others. This book shows you how to tap into this magic."

– Brian Tracy
Author of *The Way to Wealth*

"The Color of Success reinforced for me the importance of the self image in reaching goals. Mary Ellen Lapp spells out the simple steps to form a solid self image from the inside out."

– Paul Martinelli
President of LifeSuccess Consulting

"Being seen and getting noticed, two requirements of success, are presented in a new way in Mary Ellen Lapp's insightful book. The Color of Success should be required reading for everyone before they set out on their journey of success."

– Ric Thompson
Co-Founder Healthy Wealthy n Wise

"It's so simple, like attracts like, the Law of Attraction. In The Color of Success, Mary Ellen Lapp entertains and explains attraction, the magnetic force that brings success."

– Joe Vitale
Author of *The Attractor Factor and Zero Limits*

"I was shocked at the power that color has. Since reading The Color of Success, I now look in the mirror a whole new way."

– Kevin Wilke
Co-Founder Nitro Marketing

"Mary Ellen Lapp's writing paints a colorful picture of how looking good and feeling good create the masterpiece called you. The Color of Success shows you how."

– Joe Borrello
President of Tasters Guild International

"You are unique – in all the world, there is only one of YOU! Mary Ellen Lapp brings to us The Color of Success as a creative way to help you discover and highlight your very own unique self! Enjoy!"

– Carol Gates
Author of *As You Wish* and President of Coaching for LifeSuccessProductions

INTRODUCTION

"Success depends on a *plus* condition of the mind and body, on power of work, on courage. A *minus* condition cannot be continued if you hope to lead a fuller life."

– Dorthea Brande, *Wake Up and Live!*

The simplest yet most powerful way to put yourself into a plus condition is by using color to your best advantage. Color gets you noticed. Color is your signature. Color keeps you in an environment of positive movement toward your success.

HOW DO YOU CHOOSE COLOR?

WHAT DO YOUR CHOICES SAY ABOUT YOU?

Let's follow some color conscious individuals and see how their color choices work for them.

Jennifer eagerly surveys a well-stocked display table piled high with the season's newest sweaters. The colorful window displays of artfully coordinated outfits at her neighborhood Chico's store always lure her in. The soft textures and assortment of colors entice her to select several sweaters to try on. She scoops them up and hurries off to the fitting room.

The red one, the blue one, the pink, the green, each is lovelier than the last. Jennifer's shoulder length, sandy colored hair and creamy skin are perfectly suited for vibrant color. How will she make her choice?

Pam, the Chico's sales associate, helpfully comments to Jennifer as she stands before the mirror, "That one brings out the color of your eyes."

> "THAT ONE BRINGS OUT THE COLOR OF YOUR EYES."

"Hmm, she's right about that," Jennifer nods. The cerulean blue reminds her of the ocean she visited on her tropical vacation last year. Her eyes sparkle as they reflect the soothing blue.

"That's a great color with your skin tone", Pam adds as Jennifer models another sweater.

"Yes, I do feel more cheerful in this color." The chili pepper red color makes her face glow. She stands a little taller as she admires her striking reflection.

Back in the fitting room, Jennifer slowly redresses as she considers her choices. "I like them all," then she hesitantly admits, "I just don't know which color is really me."

Returning the pile of sweaters back to the display table, she quickens her pace to the checkout desk. Jennifer has a single selection in hand.

Pam is surprised as she processes the transaction. "How did you select that one?" she asks Jennifer, and muses to herself, "What is she thinking?"

Jennifer just smiles and shrugs in reply, "I wear a lot of this color." Leaving the store, shopping bag in hand, she admonishes herself and sighs, "I did it again, another beige sweater". The litany of justifications follows.

This color goes with everything.

It will never go out of style.

When I get a tan this summer, this color will look better on me.

Sound familiar? Is Jennifer just being practical by making a neutral color choice, or is she withholding from herself an opportunity for success? Is her consistent, neutral color choice a plus or a *minus* in her life?

Jack is thinking about buying a new car. He is secure in his career and feels he deserves to upgrade from his decade old sedan. For months, he has read all the trade publications, and has researched every make and model. Everyday, on the way to work, Jack notices each vehicle on the road. On his mental list, he excludes this one or adds that one as he refines his possible choices.

Finally, his search ends when he glimpses the perfect vehicle, the Lexus SC430. He snaps a picture of it with his cell phone as it speeds past. The exact look, the style, even the color he wants. Now, he's ready to make his purchase.

Saturday morning, Jack works out at the gym, and then visits the Lexus dealership. He scans the rows of vehicles searching for his ideal car. Where is it? He walks into the showroom, cell phone in hand, and confidently shows the photo image to Scott, the salesperson. "This is the car I want."

It's sleek, it's sexy, and shiny Obsidian Black.

"Great choice", Scott eagerly replies. "I have one right over here."

They walk over to the gleaming Lexus SC. The graceful, aerodynamic curves of the body, the sculptured five spoke wheel covers, the sumptuous leather interior, "It's everything you want, Jack".

Jack's eyes light up as he approaches his dream car. It's even more beautiful than he remembers. "Yes, this is the car for me." He reaches out to touch the sleek fender, and observes, "But, this one is silver".

"Mercury Metallic is the color you want, Jack", Scott insists. "Look, it's in the brochure." He pushes the elegant, glossy brochure into Jack's hands. "This is the hot, new color."

Jack confirms the image on the brochure is exactly like the car in the showroom. The silvery hue in the photograph looks dynamic in daylight and dramatic in darkness. He begins to reason with himself.

Well, if this is the hot, new color.
It is featured in the brochure.
Scott's the professional; he knows what he's talking about.
Black would be harder to keep looking shiny.

Jack nods and makes his decision, "Sold".

He finishes the paperwork, and shakes hands with Scott. "Thanks for your help." Scott presents Jack with his keys and some reassurance, "This car is really you, Jack. I know you're going to love it".

Jack eases into his new Lexus SC430. As he settles into the soft leather seat, the new car smell fills his nostrils. Jack leans back and closes his eyes. He sees himself, sitting tall, tanned, smiling, convertible top down, the wind in his hair, cruising down the highway in his shiny, new, *black* Lexus.

Wait, what happened here? Did the *plus* of owning the hot, new color car become a *minus* when compared to Jack's image of himself? What is more important, how the world sees Jack driving his new car, or how Jack sees Jack?

Marie and Nicole, friends since high school, are shopping for furniture. Now that Marie has bought a house, her old sofa, that has moved from apartment to apartment, needs to be replaced. Her new home deserves something special. She enjoys Nicole's company, so she invites her along on her search.

After visiting the third furniture store, Nicole questions Marie, "What is it that you're looking for? We've sat on so many sofas, I feel like I have calluses on my bum."

"I'll know it when I see it," Marie replies. "Let's try the store on Main Street."

After looking through the next store, walking from room to room, Marie shakes her head. "No, that's not it."

"Well, I have one more over here". They follow the salesman to another room further back into the store.

"That's it!" Marie startles the salesman and Nicole.

"Oh, Marie, you can't be serious." Nicole is shocked by Marie's selection.

"I've always wanted a red, leather sofa." Marie is all smiles.

Nicole, ever the practical friend, reminds Marie of the folly of her choice.

"That red will stick out like a sore thumb."
"It won't match anything else in the room."
"You'll get tired of that color fast, then what?"
"Besides, it's probably in the back of the store because no one else wants it."

Marie's smile begins to fade. She asked the salesman if Nicole is right.

"Well, we definitely sell more black leather sofas. It's a more classic look," he replies with an air of authority.

Marie's mind begins to question her initial excitement.

That's true. Black leather is a modern classic.
It's what's shown in all the magazines.
What was I thinking?
A red sofa- it's so not me.

The next day, Marie's black leather sofa is delivered. Nicole and Marie share some wine and toast to the first purchase for her new home. "It's a good thing I was with you yesterday," Nicole remarks, "or we would be sitting on an ugly red sofa."

Marie strokes the soft, dark leather. "Yeah, how bad would that be?" She hears a tiny voice inside her head. "Maybe, next time."

Is Marie listening to the voices outside her head instead of the one inside? Is the *plus* self she sees, a different person than the *minus* self she shows the world? Which one is real?

Success starts with how you see yourself.

The choices you make, however subtle they appear at the time, accumulate and create the person you become. Do you always pick the "safe" color choice? Do you listen to the advice of others about what is best for you? Do you simply follow the crowd and go along with the current style?

A reminder of how easy it is to fall into the habit of going along with the crowd is the old adage, "If you always do what you've always done, you'll always get what you always got." If you do something differently today, how will your life be different tomorrow? What will you "get" that you've never gotten before?

Getting to know yourself and discovering what looks and feels best for you is infinitely more satisfying and empowering than accepting automatically the choices as they are presented to you.

Put yourself in a *plus* condition of mind and body by starting now to make your best color choices to create your fuller life of success.

CHAPTER ONE
What Color Says Success?

*I*f success is a color, what color is it?

Is it a color everybody wears?

If that were true, wouldn't everyone wearing it be a success?

Is it a color rarely seen?

That would indicate success is also rarely seen. Certainly not true.

To discover the answer to this query, what color says success, first consider this question.

WHAT IS SUCCESS TO YOU?

We all have definitions of success. A restaurant is successful if it has good food and many regular customers. An actor is successful if he has a list of movie credits to his name, and perhaps an Oscar statue or two. A politician is successful when she is elected, serves her constituents well, and is re-elected.

When we look at other people, we look at their accomplishments. It's easy to assess, in our estimation, if they are successful based on what they've done. We rely on our own values for guidance, and compare how other people measure up to our standards. Or do we?

Do we use a different scale to measure the success of others than we use to gauge our own measure of success? Is success, for ourselves, always a little further away from where we are right now?

DO YOU MEASURE SUCCESS FOR YOURSELF IN QUALIFYING TERMS?

I'll be a success when I get that new job, or...

...when I reach my sales quota.
...when I get that promotion.
...when I have my own business.
...when I make my first million.
...when I get the kids through college.
...when I write a best-selling book.
...when I can retire to my mountain cabin.

I will be a success when... fill in your favorite benchmark. Success is somewhere off in the future, something to look forward to. Not quite there yet.

Realize this- success need not be an idealized future event.

WHY NOT ENJOY YOUR SUCCESS TODAY?

Eckhart Tolle in his book, *The Power of Now,* describes the human condition as "the compulsion to live almost exclusively through memory and anticipation" that creates "an endless preoccupation with past and future and an unwillingness to honor and acknowledge the present moment".

We are encouraged throughout life to make plans, set goals and learn by our mistakes. These are all necessary activities for effective time management and healthy self-improvement. Yet, if you are spending your time vacillating between reliving past mistakes and projecting yourself into the unknown future, you are ignoring who you are today.

Reminding yourself of past difficulties will only set you up for feelings of present self-doubt. Imagining future obstacles focuses you on feelings of fear in the present. In this present moment, you are the product of all your accomplishments, all your successes. Remind yourself of this truth-

"I always succeed at producing a result."

Honor and acknowledge the present moment by realizing, you are already fully equipped to live in your now.

Earl Nightingale, a lifelong observer of human potential, described success as *"the progressive realization of a worthy ideal"*. His definition of success is one that has been embraced by many of the people we classify as being successful. The most successful people throughout history have shared the belief that success occurs every day when you focus on a goal and take daily action toward reaching that goal. Reread the words in Nightingales' definition. They clearly describe success as a journey, not a destination.

"The progressive realization of a worthy ideal."

Think about each word and its meaning.
Through forward movement,
a step by step increasing in intensity,
you bring into reality,
through your time and effort,
what started as merely an idea.

You have the power to bring your thoughts into reality!

Everything around you, this book, your clothing, the furniture, the building, your city, even this country, began as an idea in someone's mind. Those thoughts, through focus and planning and toil, are now a reality.

What thoughts are creating your reality? Is your primary thought a worthy ideal?

An ideal is described as "an idea you have fallen in love with." An idea that is worth trading the hours of your life to bring it into reality had better be idea that you can love. Think about what ideas populate your mind. If your thoughts could magically become your reality, would you find yourself in the perfect place of your dreams? Or would your thoughts if manifested be your worst nightmare?

James Allen, in his often-quoted book, *As a Man Thinketh,* summarizes his message as, "We become what we think about". The magic to transform our thoughts into our reality is not magic at all. It is simply the way it works, a law of nature. Think doubtful and fearful thoughts, and you will experience more of what you are thinking. Fill your mind with thoughts of possibility and the anticipation of a positive outcome and you are headed that direction.

What you think about yourself, you become.

Brian Tracy explains it this way, "You'll never outperform your self image."

Success doesn't happen when you "get there". Success is found in what you achieve everyday. Your every thought, every idea is on its way to becoming a reality. Success begins first with your thoughts. See yourself as achieving your worthy ideal. See yourself as being the success that is within you.

> SEE YOURSELF AS BEING THE SUCCESS THAT IS WITHIN YOU.

When, as observers, we see other's outcomes that we classify as a success, we look past the inward journey that was filled with daily, or hourly, successes along the way before the outward success became apparent. By beginning with an appreciation of our own present successes, we can see more deeply into how others created success for themselves. We can then more easily emulate their positive advances to aid in our own journey.

That popular restaurant, filled with happy diners, had its first success when the proprietor dreamed of serving customers her favorite recipes, long before the tables and chairs were in place. Her idea, through organized planning, moved forward. Each day, the picture in her mind grew clearer. Each step taken, the procurement of the building, the fixtures for the kitchen, the menu selections, the financing to pay for it, they were all progressions, all successes on the way to her worthy ideal.

The Academy Award winning actor first tasted success as he starred in his own neighborhood plays on a proscenium fashioned in his garage. Each time he took the stage, his confidence and comfort level increased. With each exuberant laugh he heard, and hearty applause he earned, he realized the gift he had for performing. He never lost his worthy ideal as he continued to pursue more roles to expand his talents and fulfill his vision of himself.

The well-respected politician knew she was a success when she made it her life's work to stand up for the rights of people. When she made the decision to learn the skills of an orator, and to be mentored by people she respected, she moved forward to become the best advocate, to speak for others, and create positive change, her worthy ideal.

If you are to enjoy your own "progressive realization", your successes along the way, first put yourself in the mode to realize daily success. See yourself as the best you can be. Surround yourself with your own Color of Success.

When we observe another person, we take all of three seconds to form an impression of them. We observe height, weight, coloration, and other noticeable details. Posture, grooming, clothing, hairstyle, they are all taken in that three seconds.

The information goes in quickly, but people have a short attention span. When asked to describe a person who just walked past you, how many of your three-second observations would you recall? Chances are you will remember one thing in that short encounter. You will recall either the person's best feature or their worst.

SO WHAT GETS OUR ATTENTION? WHAT IS MEMORABLE?

Theron Dumont wrote in *The Power of Concentration*, "You make your own place, and whether it is important depends on you." This simple sentence puts the responsibility for how you are perceived squarely on you.

You cannot control what another person thinks, but you can influence what they notice. In that three-second observation window, what is noticeable about you?

We never want to admit that looks matter. In a perfect world, we are all judged solely by our character or our intelligence. The truth is, we are more likely to be blind to the character flaws of another person than any noticeable physical flaws. We live in a visual world. What we see matters.

Laura Morsch, a writer for CareerBuilder. com, quoted research published in The Journal of Labor Economics. She found that attractive people earn more and are more likely to be promoted than their average-looking counterparts are. Just look at the cover of any popular magazine. No unattractive faces or physiques found there. *People Magazine's* issue on the Most Beautiful People is a top seller. Pleasant images always beat out images that make us uncomfortable.

CONFIDENCE MAKES UP 20 PERCENT OF PERCEIVED ATTRACTIVENESS.

However, Morsch goes on to point out that the research indicates, "Fortunately, there is more to attractiveness than meets the eye. Confidence makes up 20 percent of perceived attractiveness."

That's a relief. In the world of real people, not glossy magazine images, we are attracted to charisma in people, not solely physical characteristics. Think about the most charismatic person you know, someone that you enjoy being with. Chances are he or she is not particularly handsome or beautiful. It's obvious the moment you see them, they have that special something. You are comfortable being with that person because they are comfortable with themselves. They are attractive because of an aura of confidence.

You are in charge of your place in the world. You are in control of the impression you make in your surroundings. Are you confident you are making your best impression? In that three-second window of time that everyone is allotted, you must first be noticed, before you can expect your ideas to be heard and your work to be appreciated.

WHAT IS ATTENTION GETTING? COLOR!

At an early age, color is one of the first things we notice. An infant's eyes are drawn to intense colors as they learn to focus through the contrast of light and dark color. Pale, pastel colors, traditionally selected for babies, may echo their frailty, but a baby's developing eyes prefer stronger colors, or the contrast created by black and white images.

As we mature, we never loose the lure of color. It defines and describes our world. Color speaks an inaudible language that communicates far more than our eyes see.

Advertisers realize the power of color. A signature color on a product is more memorable than any message written on the package. Color is so important in the marketing message that manufacturers routinely assemble focus groups of potential customers to determine what color packaging will entice them to buy their products.

In the book Don't Think Pink, by authors Lisa Johnson and Andrea Learned, a marketing consultant's focus group presentation is described. Since women purchase more pet food, the marketers presumed women shoppers would be more attracted to pastel pink packaging on bags of dog food. They discovered from the women in the focus group that their traditional color assumptions were incorrect. Women do not prefer pale pink, especially not on dog food packaging. By asking their target market, they were able to avoid a costly product packaging error.

Shopping in the grocery store, your eyes scan row after row of canned soups arranged on the shelves. To find what you're searching for, you look first for the color of the red label before you zone in on other information printed on the label. We are conditioned to associate a certain color with a product's identity. That identity becomes recognizable and memorable to us because of the color that is consistently used on the label.

We may be easily fooled by look-alike brands that hope to capitalize on another product's color identity. The same color, used on a similar product's packaging, has the desired effect when we inadvertently select the competing product. Not until the purchase is made and we are back home do we discover in frustration, this is not our regular brand. We accepted the message of color and automatically made our selection. The trick worked and color fooled us.

Have you ever been totally lost when the manufacturer changes the color of its packaging? "I forget the brand," you explain to the clerk, "but it has a green label." Other information may have escaped you, the brand name, even exactly, what the product does, but you haven't lost your memory of the color of the package. If a product's sales are lagging, changing the outer look may just be the attention getting answer. A new color says "a new product to try". Otherwise, a change, for change sake, can be damaging to a product's brand loyalty.

If you've ever used Carmex on your chapped lips, you recognize the small, round jar with the yellow lid. The healing combination of camphor and menthol has a distinctive smell and flavor. The packaging has remained the same for decades. The manufacturer has plans to introduce the product in other flavors, and to change the signature packaging, to keep up with market trends. Whether this is a positive business strategy or suicide for the brand, time will tell.

As a long time customer, I'm disappointed by the planned change in this icon of lip healing. It's a product I purchase by defaulting to the color message. I don't want to have to search for it amid products that are packaged all the same.

Savvy marketers capitalize on our profound color memory and reinforce their signature color by telling us to "look for the yellow label". They realize that customers look for color first, so in giving us permission to do so, we are rewarded for finding the color with the effortless discovery of their product. This brand true strategy assures there will be no color makeover in the future of this product.

Obviously, color is a great place to begin to make your own memorable impression on the world. That doesn't mean wearing a uniform of only one color. You are about to discover your signature colors. Colors you'll want to include in creating the memorable brand that is uniquely **You**.

Everyone starts with natural coloration. Your skin tone, eye color, hair color, whether it's what you were born with or not, creates the canvas onto which you add your own colors. Nature is expert at providing complementary natural coloration. Your natural born colors will always look best on you. To look your best, resist the temptation to drastically alter nature's handiwork.

> THERE ARE TIMES WHEN YOU INTUITIVELY KNOW YOU'RE WEARING YOUR BEST COLOR.

Nature has a way of adapting color as we grow older, so as hair color changes, so does the coloration of our skin tone. By ignoring your naturally changing coloration, and excessively darkening the color of your hair, your skin appears too pale in comparison. Also, if your hair and skin tone are naturally dark, yet you long to go blond, know that you will not look totally natural with a significantly lighter hair color. "You can't fool mother nature", as the advertising slogan goes. Start with the canvas of your natural coloration to discover your most flattering colors.

There are times when you intuitively know you're wearing your best color. It may be your "favorite" dress or your "lucky" sport coat. When you're wearing it, you just know you're going to have a great day. You tend to smile more. Little irritations don't bother you as much. It's as if you're wearing protective armor from the annoyances of life. Nothing holds you back.

Your self-fashioned protection from the world is a result of trusting your instincts about color. You may have stopped listening to that small voice of instinct years ago. Way back in grade school, you were encouraged to color the grass green, the sky blue. Experimentation with color, as when you painted a red sky and purple grass, was discouraged in favor of predicable combinations. The well meaning, encouragement toward conformity may have taken away your natural ability to know what looks and feels good to you.

Colors, we are taught, are identified with the sexes, pink for girls, blue for boys. A baby wrapped in a blue blanket, we just assume, a boy. A parent wouldn't dare to put a pink sweatshirt on a two year old that wasn't a girl. Traditions are formed. The rules are routinely followed. The comforting thing about rules is, once you learn them, and follow them, no further thought is required. Instead of making individual color choices, the thinking is already done.

Unless you want to always think pink, or be forever in blue, let's find out what other options you have in colors that are really **You**.

Mark Train said, "The secret of getting ahead is getting started. The secret of getting started is breaking your complex overwhelming tasks into small manageable tasks, and then starting on the first one."

ARE YOU READY TO GET STARTED ON FINDING YOUR BEST COLOR?

WILL YOU DEFY CONVENTION AND BREAK THE RULES?

Your first small task is to notice again.
What looks good on you?

As you get dressed each day, take a moment in front of the mirror.
Notice the colors you're wearing.
How does that image make you feel?
Let your intuition answer this question.
You are not being critical.
You are just being **aware.**

It doesn't matter if you're wearing the sweater given to you by Aunt Maude, the tie from your mother-in-law, or a great buy you found on the sale rack. Just notice the color of the fabric against your skin tone, next to your face, and with your hair color. What color is brought out in your eyes?

Keep a pen and paper near your mirror and make a note of what colors make you feel your best. If you see a smiling face looking back at you, you have probably picked a good color for you. You feel uplifted and happy. Make a note to try out this color on another day and see if you get the same results.

If your expression is just OK, the color may still work for you, but maybe something is missing- an accent color or accessory to liven up a just OK color. Try adding a jacket, tie, or scarf of another color and note if you see an improvement.

If you can't even crack a smile at your reflection in the mirror, that color is not doing its job. Change your clothes immediately, and try another choice. Something about the color, the feel, or the fit of what you are wearing is bringing you down. Life is too short to drink bad wine, or to look badly in your clothes. Here's a color rule you can follow. Always keep a bag or box for clothing donations nearby. There must be someone in the world that is well suited for the offending color.

What if nothing you try on gives you the desired lift in spirits? You have obviously been selecting colors that are inappropriate for you. If you have several pieces of clothing that same color, you've taken on a color identity that is not setting you up for success. The remedy is to find color that makes you feel great.

> "SUCCESS IS THE CONSTANT UNFOLDING OF YOUR SOUL."
>
> – Dr. Michael Beckwith

Author James Allen wrote, *"We think in secret and it comes to pass. Environment is but our looking glass".* The image looking back at you is the environment in which you will spend your day. An environment you create by how the color you're wearing makes you feel. That image reflects to the world how you feel about yourself.

If the color doesn't feel good, don't wear it. Even if it was a gift from your mother, don't wear it. Regardless how much you spent to buy it, don't wear it. Give it away. Make a pillow out of it. Loose it at the drycleaners. There is never a reason to wear a color that's not right for you. No reason to ever feel less than fabulous in color.

After a few days of noticing in your mirror, your awareness will begin to expand beyond your own refection. What do you notice about the person you pass on the street or a co-worker in your office? Does their color choice speak confidence? Is it flattering? What impression of them are you left with?

As you start to notice how color affects you, you will also notice how your color choices affect the people you meet. Color is the language of the emotions. Since emotions lie below conscious awareness, your color choices affect people on another level. They may not realize why.

When you enter a room, outfitted in your best color, the smile on your face is contagious. Your aura of confidence affects all you meet. Your awareness of the image you show the world brings you a greater appreciation of **how success feels**.

As Reverend Michael Beckwith believes, *"Success is the constant unfolding of your soul."* The better you feel about yourself, the easier it is for you to realize your daily successes.

Success is a do-it-yourself project.

Your success is up to you.

CHAPTER TWO
Are You Color Shy?

*C*olor dominates our visual world. Sight, for those of us gifted with this marvelous faculty, is the one sense that we rely on the most. As soon as daylight illuminates our world, we immediately notice that color surrounds us.

You open your eyes in the morning and see the bright red numbers on the black digital clock. Looking out the window for the day's weather clues, you see blue sky or gray clouds. You bury your face in the ecru pillowcase, then, remember the deep brown coffee awaiting you in the sunny yellow kitchen. Pouring the dark, steaming liquid from your silver coffee carafe into your favorite orange mug, you dribble a bit onto the green countertop. Grabbing the blue sponge from the white sink, you clean up the evidence, and down a glass of golden orange juice and toast of crispy beige bread.

Then off to shower, where bottles of yellow shampoo, green conditioner and amber soap line the almond walls. White steam fills the shower as the water bounces off your shell pink toenails. You hang up your purple scrungie, grab a navy towel to dry off and replace it on the gold towel bar. Spreading mint green toothpaste on your aqua toothbrush, you brush your pearly white teeth, then, run a red comb thru your brown hair. Looking inside your closet to select what to wear today, color again takes center stage.

The kaleidoscope of colors that surrounds you in that first few minutes of wakefulness are only a preview of what the day will bring. Color directs and affects you all day long.

COLOR'S FUNCTION IS PRIMARILY TO GET OUR ATTENTION.

From an early age, we are conditioned to recognize color as a signal. At the traffic light, we learn red means stop, yellow yield, and green to go. Orange barrels on the side of the road caution us to road construction hazards. Flashing red lights in our rear view mirror are our signal to pull over. Color's function is primarily to get our attention.

Our consciousness of color also extends to another level. Color creates cues in the sub-conscious mind as well. Think of the sub-conscious mind as your storehouse of every thought and experience you've ever had. Every fact you memorized for a test, the information from every book you've read, the name of every person you have ever met, all that data is filed away in your sub-conscious mind.

With a capacity larger than any computer processor, the information input through your five senses is automatically stored in the sub-conscious mind. The sound of your mother's voice is there. The exhilaration felt from your first roller coaster ride. The tempting aroma of your grandmother's home baked cookies, as well as their delicious flavor. All memories are filed, a bazillion gigabits of memory.

When you want to retrieve a bit of information, to remember someone's name, you click on your internal search function, and amazingly, the information is found. Sometimes, it is days later, but the information is eventually retrieved. If you try to consciously think of someone's name, you may be met with frustration. The information is no longer stored in your conscious, thinking mind. It's in the archives, the sub-conscious memory.

This efficient, automatic system of the sub-conscious constantly monitors our environment as well as all of the body's functions. In addition to storing all the information that the conscious mind has accumulated our entire life, it also houses our emotions.

Color signals in the sub-conscious, though not obvious to our conscious mind, also get our attention and affect how we feel about color. Since feelings, more than sight, are at the root of all actions, we must associate a feeling with a color experience before it moves us to action. At some point in our early training, we were taught to feel a sense of alarm and urgency at the sight of a red light. We see the color red, we feel the urgency, then, take the action to stop in our tracks. Feelings associated with color determine the meaning we give it and the resulting action we take.

The conscious mind is reserved for thought, and so we spend much of our time there, thinking about or processing the input. When you decide which color shirt to buy, you use your thinking mind to weigh your options.

Looking through a clothing rack of shirts, you are encouraged to try one on in the new color of the season. Your first thought is, "Do I already have a shirt this color?" You scan your memory bank, clothing section, for that information. Is it the same color? Lighter? Darker? What else do I have that will go with it? Your conscious mind answers these questions.

Next thought, "Is the sales clerk just telling me it looks flattering on me?" You consciously access your people perception area for a read on his sincerity. Another shopper echoes his compliment, so it must be true.

Decisions based on conscious thought are objective. Based on facts alone, decisions are, as the saying goes, black and white. However, when a color choice is involved, we don't stop there. We also use that other part of the mind.

Packed away, just out of reach of our conscious mind, are those "feelings" we have about color. Those memories about color that we received as early conditioning are filed away in the vast storehouse of our sub-conscious. Feelings provide a shortcut to decision making. We no longer have to think about what the red light means. We stop automatically.

WHAT OTHER AUTOMATIC DECISIONS ABOUT COLOR DO YOU MAKE?

Back to the decision of whether or not to buy that shirt, the facts are these. You do not already own a salmon colored shirt. It would coordinate well with your navy slacks. The sales clerk is someone you like and you trust his opinion about clothing. It's a great new color that looks good on you. The conscious facts indicate that you should add the shirt to your wardrobe.

SO, WHAT IS STOPPING YOU?

WHAT IS THAT FEELING YOU HAVE AS YOU LOOK IN THE MIRROR?

It has everything to do with a color memory. As an eight year old, your mother dressed you in a new shirt that you remember as being very similar to this color. She was so proud of how you looked. Arriving at school, you were teased all day by your peers about wearing a "pink" shirt. You made up your mind to never wear a colorful shirt again. Thirty years later, in your closet are only white and pale blue shirts.

Maybe you haven't thought about that experience in thirty years. Standing in front of the mirror, wearing that shirt, your color memory evoked an unpleasant feeling. You may not even know why, but you hung the shirt back on the rack. The accumulated information hidden away in your subconscious mind determines if you are comfortable with color, or if you are color shy. Early experiences with color hold the clues.

As with all experiences in life, they have created the person you are today. Now that you are old enough to make your own decisions, it's up to you to determine if the feelings you have resulting from an early experience still serve you today.

You are your own person now. What an eight-year-old thought about your shirt thirty years ago is of no consequence today.

Embrace the good feelings you have about a color. Pay attention to the automatic negative reactions a color brings out in you. You're not eight years old anymore. Break through your resistance by trying the color in a small way. Buy the shirt and gage the reaction of adult peers you trust. Don't withhold from yourself an opportunity for success by reliving the past. Change your mind about it.

Look at the colors in nature. From some divine plan, nature's colors are always perfectly coordinated. We never say the yellow of the dandelion doesn't complement the green of the grass. Or that the blue of the ocean and the blue of the sky aren't well matched. A rainbow blends all colors together, yet they never seem to clash. Nature effortlessly mixes and matches colors with great success.

SO WHY ARE WE CHALLENGED TO COORDINATE THE COLORS OF A TIE WITH A SHIRT?

WHY ARE WE FRUSTRATED WHEN TRYING TO FIND SOMETHING TO MATCH THAT NEW SKIRT?

Nature's color palette begins with a definite purpose. The brightly colored cardinal effectively attracts its mate. The ever-changing chameleon uses color to disappear. The humming bird is drawn to brightly colored blooms. Animal and plant species use color for attraction and survival. So what can color accomplish for you?

Everyone has his own individual atmosphere. As each flower has its distinctive aroma, we each have things about us that make us memorable. One of those things is color. What we see, we remember. Color is what we most easily see. Describe the person across the room from you. Invariably you will mention the color of their complexion, clothing, eyes, or hair. If you're extremely attuned, perhaps you'll notice the color of their energy field as an aura surrounding them. All of these colorful attributes create your personal atmosphere.

You create the *colorscape* around you. The colors you wear, the colors you surround yourself with in your home, your work area, even the vehicle you drive are a result of you actively choosing your environment.

Don't remember picking the brown carpet in your living room? Making no choice is also a choice. Your own indecision may have left that choice to someone else. When you voiced no opinion, perhaps your spouse, decided on the color for both of you.

Peer pressure may have affected your color opinion. Friends down the street also have brown carpet. You've seen it in all the decorating magazines. Brown is what's popular. That provides the social proof, brown is a good choice.

Or was it your comfort zone that influenced your color choice? The old carpet you just replaced was also brown. It's the color you've always had. You're used to it. It's practical, doesn't show the dark pet hair.

Whatever the reason, you have new brown carpet. Nothing wrong with brown, unless you really don't like brown. Does the color remind you of the scrap of carpeting in the neighborhood clubhouse? You remember a time, when as a young child, the older kids wouldn't let you join. Kept out of that clubhouse, you were an outsider. Humph! Who wants to be part of their dumb club anyway? You pouted for days.

One of those color memories, just out of reach of your conscious mind, but now you scowl every time you walk into that room with the brown carpet. You feel you just don't belong there. You have a choice to make. You can wallow in those uncomfortable brown feelings and avoid that room. You can change your mind about how you feel about brown. Or, you can find another carpet color.

AS IN NATURE, COLOR ATTRACTS LIKE A MAGNET.

Businessman, philanthropist and author, W. Clement Stone said, *"Be careful the environment you choose for it will shape you. So choose the environment that will best develop you toward your objective. Analyze your life in terms of its environment. Are the things around you helping you toward success - or are they holding you back?"*

To control your own colorscape, your environment, first become comfortable with color and what colors mean to you. Learn how color evokes a mood. Discover your own best colors, and surround yourself with the colors that are right for you.

As in nature, color attracts like a magnet. Our predominant color preference draws us in. On a sunny day, you reach for the yellow shirt. On a rainy day, you wear the blue one. Why is that? You want to wear what you are feeling. We are naturally drawn to what we feel. You listen to mellow music when you're feeling low or jazzy tunes when you're up.

The feelings created by our sub-conscious associations with color are always in control unless we consciously overrule them. Where you are in your life today, you may be drawn to a more colorful environment, but your subconscious color conditioning is holding you back. Trapped in a comfort zone that is impeding your progress. It is our sub-conscious feelings, not simply conscious thoughts, that propel us to action or keep us stuck where we are.

Feel good about color and color will keep you feeling good. Notice what colors attract you. What does that color attraction say about you? Are you drawn to a color, yet not giving yourself permission to wear it or live with it? Your level of confidence, your decisiveness, your values, are all manifested through color. If you're holding yourself back from color, that's also the image you show to the world.

Colors are individual choices. Who picks the colors around you? Do you leave your color environment up to a spouse, or do you follow the latest color trend? Someone else's selections made for you, or the dictates of what's in vogue may not be serving you. Tangerine may be the color of the day, but not your day. Trust your own opinions.

Select your colorscape yourself.

HOW DO YOU BEGIN TO CONTROL THE COLORS IN YOUR WORLD?

WHERE DO YOU START?

Start in your closet.

What colors do you see? This will be easier if you take the time to arrange your clothing by color. If you have patterns with multiple colors, choose the main color. If you have a strong color preference already, this step may not be necessary. The predominant color of your wardrobe will jump out at you.

This is your current color identity. When someone describes seeing you, they will mention you as wearing this color. You are consistent in the choice of this color, but owning a lot of a color does not guarantee it is the best choice for you. You may routinely pick a safe color, beige or black, that does nothing to reflect the real you.

If you see a variety of colors, this indicates you are still experimenting with finding a color identity. Your selections are based on what's available rather than searching out a specific color. Color is not your prime buying motivator. By noticing how the different colors look on you, you'll be able to weed out some ordinary colors and only wear your best ones.

Does your closet look like a rainbow? If you like to pick the most colorful choice, you already love color. Chances are there are several colors in your closet that should be eliminated. Not all colors are flattering on you and the sooner you eliminate those, the more space you'll have for your best colors.

Do you notice a coordination of similar colors, like cool blues and greens, or warm reds and rusts? Are there neutral color families, like beige and brown? You have a tendency toward a monochromatic color direction. If those choices are flattering, feel good colors, you are well on your way to finding good colors for you.

For your next clue into your color identity, look at the color of the car you drive.

Especially in America, cars are an extension of personality. Many of your waking hours are spent in this portable environment. Cars become a second home complete with the conveniences of comfortable reclining seats, audio and video entertainment, refreshment stations and non-stop communication anywhere you travel. Why wouldn't you want your home away from home to reflect your personality?

SO, WHAT DOES THE COLOR OF YOUR CAR SAY ABOUT YOU?

ARE YOU A CONFORMIST?

Do you drive the most popular color? You reason, someone decided for me the car colors from which to choose. The color shown in the magazines, on television, and in the product brochures must be the best color. That's why they feature it. Nice of them to decide the best one for you. So, that's why you buy it.

For six years running, that means a majority car buyers have been driving a silver car. DuPont, the world's leading supplier of color coatings to the automotive industry, creates the colors that are featured on eight of the top 10 selling vehicles in the United States. In their annual DuPont Automotive Color Popularity Report, consumers have consistently chosen silver most often.

The color silver represents technology and the future. Space ships were always pictured in silver. Silver is cutting edge and shiny. Because of its popularity, it's also a "safe" color in terms of resale value.

DuPont cites recent information that silver's popularity may be waning. Consumers are ready to make a change. "The auto market is further pushing the envelope in color, recognizing that as many as 40 percent of consumers are likely to switch brands if they can't get the color they want," said Karen Surcina, color marketing and technology manager for DuPont Automotive Systems.

Color is an important buying factor. As cars become an even more significant part of everyday life, rather than playing it safe, some consumers have chosen to become...

An Individualist.

There's not another car like yours on the road. You don't want to simply blend into the highway, so you look for the unique, the rare, the unusual color.

In answer to this consumer preference, DuPont's Surcina observes, "we see more of a 'notice me' effect in the choice of brighter colors– people are becoming more optimistic, they're proud of their new car and want to be seen".

Red, yellow and orange, crayon bright colors are meant for you. Or the optical illusion creating metallic and pearlescent effects of the new reds, blues and purples that, by design, are attention getting. In DuPont's view, "New pigment combinations, including those that create a hue-shift based on the viewing angle, will allow greater freedom for creating new, distinctive color spaces".

What's popular doesn't matter? Neither does standing out. You're Practical.

The color car you choose doesn't show the dirt or the dents. Your car is first and foremost transportation. Color only matters if it means ease of care. It's light brown, or gray for you.

Noticing color may be a challenge for you because, up until now, you've never really thought about color as affecting you one way or another. It's just a color, like the ground, like the sand, like your pants and your shoes. Practical and serviceable.

In some instances, the color choice for the vehicle is a joint decision or even a compromise. What if an individualist and a pragmatist share the portable color environment of the vehicle? For now, we're exploring your color personality, so what color would you choose if it were only your decision? How do you want to be seen?

We've looked at your clothing, your car. Where else does color surround you?

HOW DOES COLOR AFFECT YOUR HOME LIFE?

Colors used in your home can create your cocoon, your refuge. Color can also feel unwelcoming and make you feel ill at ease. Again the question, what does the color feel like to you? Are there rooms in your home where you don't feel comfortable? You can't explain why, you just don't spend much time there. Color may be the reason.

> OUR EMOTIONAL RESPONSES TO COLOR ARE THE COLOR LESSONS STORED IN THE SUB-CONSCIOUS.

Yellow is widely considered to be a cheerful color, but there are also claims that yellow causes irritation. Couples fight more in yellow kitchens. Babies cry more frequently when put in yellow rooms. Agitating the mind by brainstorming on a yellow legal pad may be a great way to generate ideas, but use another color notepad if your goal is negotiation. Try it for yourself. How does yellow affect you?

Blue is a cool, soothing color, and frequently used in bedrooms to promote relaxation and sleep. Like a placid lake, it is calming and serene. So, if your love life is lacking, then blue is sending the wrong message. It's time to add some fiery color to uplift your spirits. Reds are warm and mood enhancing. Dark colors rather than pale pastels are cozy at night.

Our emotional responses to color are the color lessons stored in the sub-conscious. When being around a color feels good to you, you are surrounded with a life affirming color. What colors do you remember fondly from your childhood?

What color were the walls of your first bedroom? This room meant early independence, your own special place to play and imagine. Remember how different the color looked first thing in the morning as the sunlight peeked through the curtains, compared to the last rays of dusk that shadowed the walls with a deeper color? This comfortable memory may still draw you to that color.

Think about the colors that surround you now. Is your home stark or is it a colorful, creative space? Is it cozy or confining? It's helpful to learn from design professionals about the options available to you. The suitability of fabrics, the room layout, and furniture designs are all considerations that require guidance.

Your home environment is meant to nurture you. You know which colors feel good to you. Make your preferences known to your designer. The selections available in home décor today are endless. The colors you enjoy most can easily be translated by a professional designer into an environment that suits you and is an attractive space that feels like home.

WHAT ABOUT ENVIRONMENTS WHERE YOU'RE NOT GIVEN A CHOICE?

WHAT ABOUT THE COLORS AT WORK?

The workplace may not provide you many opportunities for color selection. Awareness of the colors around you and their impact on you is the key. Color in the workplace may have more impact than color at home due to the hours spent in one place, doing one thing, which defines many jobs.

Since long-term color exposure affects your productivity and safety pay attention to your environment. Color can contribute to eyestrain, especially where computer work is done.

A bright wall, like white or yellow, used behind a computer screen will overly stress the eyes, just as having bright light from a window. It is more comfortable to create a contrast with a darker color behind the brightness of the monitor. If it's not possible to change the wall color, try angling the screen or adding a darker bulletin board behind it. Take a break each hour away from your desk, and look at a darker color to readjust your eyes.

Attitude is clearly linked to the colors that surround us. Dark colors in a small office space or cubicle will feel confining. More light, like a colorful desk lamp will help. By adding a little color variety, a bulletin board, picture frames, or colored mouse pad you'll feel a psychological lift. Even multi-colored, stick on notes are uplifting doses of color in addition to memory joggers.

If the colors of your workplace are uninspiring, you can create a dynamic colorscape in the work environment by your own presence. Complementary, flattering, color affects how we are seen by those around us. By wearing and surrounding yourself by your best, life-enhancing colors, you show to the world that you know who you are. You're comfortable with who you are. And you're going places!

Now that you have scrutinized the colors in your closet, the car you drive, the colors in your home and what you see at work, what does it all mean? Before we examine the consequences color choice has for you, begin by living confidently in the realm of color. First, know the language of color.

Think of a rainbow with row upon row of color. One color seems to morph into the next. Red lightens to orange, then to yellow, which becomes green on its way to blue, then on to violet before starting back at red. The **color wheel** found inside the back cover of this book is a helpful visual aid to see color's progression.

How do colors relate to one another visually? All color begins with the three, pure, or **primary colors**, red, blue and yellow. Every other color is created by mixing combinations of these three colors. Remember grade school art class mixing dollops of color together to create a new color? Colors in between the primary colors, as in our rainbow example, orange, green and purple, are created this way. They are called **secondary** colors.

Combining secondary colors together creates **tertiary** colors. The combinations to create new colors are endless, but all variations of color begin quite simply.

The addition of white to a color creates a **tint** or paler version of the color. By adding black, a darker color or **shade** is created. The lightness or darkness of a color is called its **value**. And **hue** is but another word for color at its brightest **intensity**.

YOU ARE ABOUT TO AMAZE YOURSELF.

Look at the color wheel and notice which colors are directly across from each other. Those two colors, red and green for example, are called **complementary** colors. Rather than a compliment such as, you look nice today, these colors are complements, and the colors complete each other.

You now know more about color than the average, color shy person.

Your color confidence, as you enter into a new relationship with color, will enhance your life experience. You are about to amaze yourself.

CHAPTER THREE
What is Color?

*I*t's 7:15 Monday morning. You must have forgotten to set the alarm clock! Rushing through your normal routine, you quickly shower, then, rummaging through the sock drawer, you pull out two socks. Next, you reach into the dimly lit closet, pull out a pair of pants, a shirt, and slip on your shoes. You're good to go. Grabbing your travel mug of steaming coffee, you're off to work.

At the office, you catch a few sideways glances. Are you living the nightmare of showing up for work in your pajamas? Not quite. In the unforgiving brightness of the office lighting, you're suddenly aware that your pants are dark blue, one sock is gray, the other green, your shoes are brown and your shirt a colorful print of red and green.

How could this be? You were confident, even in the morning rush, your pants, socks and shoes matched and all looked fine with the print of your shirt.

What went wrong? Have you been struck with sudden color blindness? No. You have only come to realize that color has everything to do with light.

Indeed, color, without the presence of light, does not exist.

Remember the age-old question, if a tree falls in the forest, and no one is there to hear it, does it make a sound? You can argue the answer, yes and no. Sound vibration becomes audible when it strikes the eardrum. Light is also vibration. Color becomes visible when light's vibrations, carried in waves, are captured and seen by the eye.

How we see color begins with in the remarkable laboratory within the eye. Our eyes are designed to convert experiences of light into signals that are transmitted to the brain by nerve impulses. Much like a camera lens focuses light to create an image; the lens of our eye focuses light onto the sensitive retina.

Receptors in the retina contain 250,000 color-decoding cones. Light travels through space in waves. The cones vary in their sensitivity to different waves of light, allowing us to see 7,000,000 different colors. The eye captures the light and projects it as color onto the screen of our mind.

Without light, in total darkness, the eye does not pick up any light signals. Since the only stimuli that the eye deals with is light, it becomes clear that light is itself a carrier of color information.

Imagine yourself in grade school science class. The teacher suspends a crystal clear, multi-faceted prism on a delicate thread before the wondering eyes of you and your classmates. It twirls freely in front of the classroom window, capturing everyone's rapt attention. Magically, as the sun's rays contact the prism's surface, the colors of the rainbow fall and dance across the room.

Ooh! Aahh!

What caused this magical phenomenon? Where did the colors come from? How can a clear prism create a rainbow of colors?

This was your first scientific lesson in the origin of color. It showed you that color is not always apparent. It is through the introduction of light that we can see it.

When white light passes through a prism it is separated into six distinct light rays, called the "colors of the spectrum". They are the same colors that can be seen when the suns' light is passed through raindrops. The resulting peculiar phenomenon we experience as a rainbow traversing the sky.

LIGHT ENERGY, THE ENERGY THAT ALLOWS US TO SEE COLOR, IS THE ONLY LIFE SUSTAINING ENERGY.

Light energy, the energy that allows us to see color, is the only life sustaining energy. Every other form of energy rays are damaging to the human organism. Plants are drawn to the light source and require light for photosynthesis. Humans, without artificial light sources, are naturally active in daylight and rest during darkness. We are designed to bask in the light, the same light that serves us well as we select our wardrobe.

Let's go back to your closet and see what occurred on that ill-fated morning. Due to the amount of light your eye had to work with, the 60-watt bulb in your closet, the retina did its best to collect the available light and transfer it as color information to your brain. Why did you see the colors differently than how they appeared at the office?

The human brain naturally corrects its perception of color so that the relationship of colors does not seem to change significantly even in light that is not evenly balanced in color. Meaning, we don't always see what we get. This effect, called color constancy, is a form of adaptation in which the eye and brain adjust to ambient conditions bringing them into a form of color that is understandable. We see what we are looking for.

Think about it as the "sunglasses effect". Look at the color of a red apple. When you put on sunglasses, the apple still looks red, even though the amount of light the eye receives is significantly reduced by the tint of the sunglasses. The brain knows the apple is red, even though, with sunglasses, it doesn't appear to be as red. It's the red the brain remembers. That's the color constancy of the brain.

Looking at a new object, one you have never seen before, you may have to remove the sunglasses to get a clear read on what color it really is, compared to what color you are seeing the with reduced light.

As we learned with the prism, light contains a spectrum of six colors. An object becomes visible in light because the surface of the object absorbs all colors of light except the color that is reflected back to your eye. The apple absorbs all colors of light except red, the color you see.

Your sock drawer contained various dark colors of socks. Light was absorbed by their dark surfaces. The amount of light that was reflected back to your eye by the dark fabrics was not easily discernable. Your brain's color constancy interpreted the dark gray and dark green as the same color in the dim light.

Also contributing to the discrepancy is the type of lighting. Two colors may be a virtually perfect match under dimmer incandescent light, but become a mismatch under brighter daylight. This is because the two colors were made using different colorants or dyes. The various colorants reflect light differently, giving each one a different reflectance curve in the wave of light. Whenever two colors appear to match but do not share the same curve, a metameric match exists.

That's why it's impossible to perfectly match the same color on different types of fabrics. The same blue dye looks different on wool socks than on cotton socks. Even dyed to match shoes though close in color, are never exact if the fabric content is different.

Back in your closet, you saw the pants as black because the available light from the dim overhead bulb was absorbed into their surface rather than reflecting sufficient light back to your eye to reflect the true, dark blue color. More light is reflected by lighter colors. Black reflects only 5%, while white surfaces reflect about 80% of the light.

The two colors in the print of your shirt , red and green, are complementary colors, colors found across from each other on the color wheel (refer to the inside back cover of this book). Complementary colors, when used closely together, are blended together by the eye. In the small-scale print of your shirt, red and green, blended together, create what appears to be a variation of brown. Just as when you combined too many colors together in art class, the result was a muddy brown pool of paint.

The cure for unwanted wardrobe surprises is to add more light in your closet. Double-check your color selections in natural daylight. And remember to set your alarm clock.

We experience the physiology of color as the process that takes place during our visual perception of color. What happens beyond that, the psychology of color, includes the sensation our brains make out of those perceptions.

Raymond Holliwell in *Working with the Law* compared our eyes to a pair of windows with a reflector sending images to the brain. He writes, "If the picture is a common one our memory accepts it readily, but if we are looking upon some new picture, some new scene, our memory does not recognize it, and then we must repeat the picture over and over many times until it makes a lasting impression. Therefore, we do not see with our eyes; we see with our mind."

The brain is the hub where color data from the eye is processed. Once we "see with our mind", the mind's processes can be found throughout our physical being. The cells of recognition that we rely on to make sense of what we see, are cells found everywhere the physical body. Seeing color is only the beginning of the color experience.

To illustrate how the mind processes what we see, visualize the top half of your head as your conscious mind. Your conscious mind is your thinking mind. Most of the awareness of your physical environment occurs through your conscious mind. You collect the data with the help of your five physical senses, sight, touch, hearing, smell, and taste. Your conscious mind then creates a picture on the screen of your mind.

You see the red apple. You touch the smooth curvature of its shape. You hear the crack of the knife as you cut through the skin. You smell the sweetness of the fruit. You taste the flavorful reward. Your conscious mind has a clear image of what is an apple. That image created in the mind involves your whole physiology in the apple experience. The next time you want the apple experience, you don't need to see another apple. Think apple and there it is, on the screen of your mind.

All animal species use these same physical senses to give meaning to their world. A horse has an appreciation for the apple experience. Your dog, when he sees a ball, translates that image into fierce tail wagging and the desire to play.

"IMAGINATION IS MORE IMPORTANT THEN KNOWLEDGE"

What sets humans apart from the rest of the animal kingdom, are the intellectual faculties that we call upon to understand our physical world. The intellectual faculties add the detail and rich dimension to our view of what we see. These six special talents give us our humanness, yet for many, they are infrequently used.

As you read the sensory-rich, apple experience paragraph, did you turn the words on the page into a mental picture? You saw a red apple on the screen of your mind, you felt its round shape, heard the crack of the knife as it was being cut, smelled the sweet aroma, and your mouth began to water as you tasted the apple. But there was no apple. This all happened in your mind.

The apple became real to you as you used your **imagination**, one of your intellectual faculties. Imagination was something you used often as a child. Remember lying on your back on a grassy hill and studying the clouds in the sky? You saw faces and animal shapes, as your imagination was free to create another world out of the fluffy white formations.

Now, as adults, we live in a world of realities, of what "is". But, when we allow our minds to think about what we "want to be", we let imagination back into our lives. As Einstein said, "Imagination is more important then knowledge". Look around you. The chair, the window, the building you're in, everything you see in the world today began as an idea spawned from someone's imagination. Were it not for imagination, we would not travel in planes, read by electric lights, or communicate with the help of a computer. Anything you see in its physical form started as an imagined idea. Ideas are the most valuable currency in the world. Let your intellectual faculty of imagination produces an abundant supply for you.

When you created the mental picture of the apple, you were able to keep it in your mind by focusing with your **will**, another intellectual faculty. The will is the key to accomplishment in any area of your life. When you decide on an action to take, you use your will to focus your attention there. The focus of your will creates the top of mind awareness necessary to see a project through.

Whatever you focus on in your mind expands into your physical world. Do you remind yourself of what's gone wrong in the past and dwell on the reasons why you shouldn't tackle a new challenge? Are you focused on what you **don't want** to happen instead of imagining the infinite possibilities of what you **do want**? Remember the mouth-watering image of the apple. The picture in your mind, the focus on that image, began to create in physical form, the apple experience.

As Stella Mann said, "If you hold it in your head, you'll hold it in your hand."

Your thoughts create your experience.

The other intellectual faculties, you use everyday to help you make decisions. Your **perception** tells you that a red apple means it's ripe. Perception determines what you notice about the people you meet. Their perception of you, right or wrong, becomes who you are to them. Is the image you portray the real you? Perception is the reality of the mind.

Your ability to **reason** helps you determine your preferences and to make a choice. Do you prefer the red, Delicious apple, or the green, Granny Smith apple? Reason helps you to weigh the options and to make the best selection. Through reason, you are able to question if the way you've always done something is still serving your best interests today. Were you raised with reminders of "don't speak unless spoken to" and "don't call attention to yourself"? You now are able to use your reason and know that by doing a disappearing act; you will not be seen as a person of success.

You use your **memory** of how each apple variety tasted to you in the past. Memory creates a log of useful information. It's an easy access to your past successes to remind you of your future capabilities.

Your **intuition** tells you that a freshly picked apple will taste better than one that has been in storage all winter. Intuition is that little voice that tells you to turn left instead of right, and avoiding the scene of an accident. It tells you to stop for gas today and tomorrow you find the price is higher. Call it your guardian angel, or a gut feeling, intuition is the sixth sense that determines our reactions to people and their intuition about us colors how we come across to them.

When you combine these intellectual faculties with your physical senses, your conscious mind enjoys a richer experience of your environment. You can appreciate the beauty of a sunset, and feel comfortable knowing that tomorrow you'll see the sunrise again. That vivid and colorful experience of your world becomes linked with the other half of your mind, the subconscious mind.

Visualize the other half of your mind, below your conscious mind, as the subconscious mind. That is where your feelings and emotions are housed. The subconscious mind is where you'll find your feelings about color. When color evokes a mood in you, it is your subconscious mind that's in control.

You wake up to see a gray sky outside your window. Your subconscious mind sets up the scenario before your conscious mind knows what's happening. You get out of bed a little more slowly. Your eyes are drooping. You reach into your closet and put on a blue shirt. There's no conscious reason for your gray mood, is there? It's just how your subconscious mind is advising you to feel.

Your morning commute is filled with erratic drivers that cut you off and get in your way. You struggle to find a parking place. You drop your briefcase in a puddle as you juggle your keys and coffee cup. What a day you're having!

At lunchtime, you leave the dreariness of your office, the ringing telephones and your irritating co-workers. Without much conscious thought, you walk down the block and into Jose's, a local restaurant. A subconscious salsa craving must have drawn you there.

> ATTITUDE IS ALWAYS THE COMPOSITE OF YOUR THOUGHTS, YOUR FEELINGS AND YOUR ACTIONS.

The walls are painted golden yellow with accents of bright terra cotta red. Your mood suddenly improves. It was a color craving that guided you there. You are surrounded by color that, somewhere in your subconscious mind, holds a pleasant memory. Warmth, vacation, delicious food. Whatever the color cues, your subconscious mind again takes control of your attitude. You no longer see a gray day.

Terry Trucco explains the power of our sub-conscious to create the environment we need. "The colors we crave are often a direct reaction against those that surrounded us most recently." Positive color feelings have transformed your attitude and your experience of the day.

Attitude is always the composite of your thoughts, your feelings and your actions. This trio is always responsible for producing your results. Let's look at how closely the three are linked.

Your sense of sight notified your conscious mind the morning sky was grey. The subconscious mind, the seat of the feelings, is most alert upon awakening. It associated the grey sky with a feeling of being down. Perhaps as a child, you heard "grey days are depressing" and out of habit you react this way. The conscious mind, the thinking mind, went along with the feeling, as it usually does, and produced thoughts to create the down feeling.

Thoughts – feelings – actions – results.

You say to yourself (thought), "I'm so tired". You are less energetic (feeling). You move more slowly (action). You're running late for work (result).

"I don't want to be noticed today." You feel insignificant. You pick the blue shirt. You don't plan on accomplishing much today.

"These drivers are out to get me." You feel aggressive and weave and cut through traffic, narrowly escaping being the cause of an accident.

"There's never enough parking." You feel out of control and find no place to park in the closest parking lot. Now you're very late for work.

"I really need to clean out this briefcase." You feel disorganized. Kerplunk! You drop it into a puddle. You'll have to redo the report inside.

"I work with a bunch of incompetents." You feel trapped by your job and scowl as you answer the phone. A good customer comments to your boss about your poor attitude.

"I need a change of scenery." You feel the need to escape and leave for lunch earlier than normal. You breathe a sigh of relief as you are drawn to a positive dose of color that improves your outlook.

Each thought you created in your conscious mind, reinforced the first feeling by the subconscious mind that morning. Your thoughts determined the actions you took, and those actions manifested as the results you experienced. A good day, or a bad day, is entirely up to you.

I know what you're thinking.

"Does every cloudy morning mean I'm in for a bad day?"

That's true, only if you allow a negative, subconscious color memory to affect your conscious state. You are in control of the thoughts you think. Only you can allow a thought to take up residence in your mind.

The subconscious mind, where color memories reside, finds expression through you in feelings and actions. Any thought that you impress over and over becomes fixed in the subconscious as a habit. Do gray days habitually cause you to feel down? Habits are expressed through you as actions. Habits are what you do everyday **without thinking about it.**

How else could you respond to a gray day? Instead of not thinking about it, like the force of habit, **think about it.** When you are feeling down, ask yourself, "Why am I feeling down?"

What is the **thought** that is creating this **feeling?**

Is that thought based on your **reality,** or doubts from the past and fears of the future? Is it a thought you grew up with that now has no relevance for the person you are today?

Introduce the power of conscious thought. Remember to use your intellectual faculties. Let's take another look at the cloudy grey morning.

The **perception** of your mood is your cue to think from where the feeling is coming. Just an irrelevant, habitual thought, you choose to not think it. Be good to yourself today.

There is no logical **reason** not to feel great today. It's only the weather condition, not yours.

USE YOUR WILL TO FOCUS ON WHAT YOU WILL ACCOMPLISH TODAY.

Access your **memory** for something that makes your feel good. Positive memories far outnumber the negative ones. Remember jumping in the puddles?

You are able to **imagine** the sky brilliant blue. Just above the clouds, it still is. Start imagining where your next flight will take you.

Intuition tells you that by wearing a bright color today, your mood will improve. And by going to the second parking lot, there will always be a place to park.

Use your **will** to focus on what you will accomplish today.

Before you leave home, your day is back on the right track. The inconveniences and irritations that you habitually experienced with your old way of thinking won't be a part of your day. Awareness is the first step in creating new thoughts, positive feelings, and more productive actions that lead to the results you want.

Your experience of color follows the same thought, feeling, action and result progression. The existence of color, noticed first by our physical senses, is appreciated with the help of our intellectual faculties. We use perception to evaluate a color's suitability, or memory to relate it to a color we've seen. The impact of color goes much deeper. Erupting from the sub-conscious are our feelings, colorful feelings.

If you have a strong color preference, it means your subconscious mind has a positive memory associated with that color. That memory causes you to select it over and over again. In your clothing, your home, your car, your preferred color is always comfortable for you, always inviting. Like Pavlov's dogs, you are rewarded with good feelings each time you see your favorite color.

Given a choice, I always pick red. Notice the color of this book. It's the emotional attachment. I'll tell you why in a later chapter.

Color, as it is depicted in art, creates an emotional response. Especially in abstract images, the combination of colors speaks to us on a level we cannot explain. The art may not be representational of anything recognizable, but it is supremely pleasing. The presentation of color without the distraction of recognizable form, the mind is free to interpret the color message directly in the sub-conscious.

Quoting internationally renowned artist, Simon Bull, "My work used to be dependent on what I was looking at. Now it's more dependent on what I am not looking at. Color eventually became my subject matter. It didn't matter if the content was a vase of flowers or a landscape or an abstract...it all turned into more background and the color itself became foreground. Now I can communicate an emotion or a feeling in a much more powerful way than by painting something just in the way I see it with my eyes."

He describes his affinity to color, "It's incredibly energizing and liberating to make marks in color that come alive and work together to express something that touches people and makes them feel good, cleansed, invigorated and uplifted."

It's the color freedom we enjoyed as children, from its origins in the spinning prism to the painting of red sky and purple grass. Color is light, color is emotion. Color explains who we are.

CHAPTER FOUR
Colorful Culture

As common and pervasive as color is in our lives today, imagine a time when the use of color was limited. Before store shelves arrayed plastic cups in rainbow hues and clothing racks presented selections of coats of any color, the production of colored goods was not so simple, or so common.

In ancient times, dyes and pigments were rare. Colors were produced by using natural dyes, like indigo and magenta. Or by the use of pigments found in the earth, such as cadmium or cobalt. Extracting dyes from vegetable sources or mining them from the earth took time and energy. Necessary activities such as growing food and building shelter took priority over color production.

Colors today are not always created from their natural sources. These original color names are still familiar to painters, but are rarely used in describing hues today. Colors are chemically produced more easily and with much more variety.

The common fabrics of centuries past, linen, flax, cotton and wool, were used in their natural colorations. It was unimportant to change the color of a thing, since color had no bearing on its usefulness. It was perfectly suitable to use the fiber the way it grew naturally. No matter that everyone wore the same color cloak. Color was not yet tied to personal identity or fashion. Decorative color had other meanings.

Pigments were so precious they were used as currency for trade or given as valued gifts. The scarcity and early significance of color indicated that only the wealthy could afford to use color. We see evidence of the use of strong colors as preserved in the ancient tombs of Egyptian nobles. The stronger the dye used, the greater the sign of wealth and importance.

Color associations we have today, such as deep purple being linked with royalty, had their beginnings from the limited use of this deeply saturated color. Cleopatra, it is rumored, needed 20,000 snails, soaked for ten days, to obtain one ounce of purple dye for her royal clothing.

Increasing trade with other parts of the world introduced unusual dyes, and produced different colors than were commonly seen in Europe and America. Deep, saturated hues brought from India and China introduced the Western world to uncharacteristically intense color.

Fashion loved the color rich silks from the East. The smooth, iridescent fabric reflected the light and caused the colors to glow intently. This graceful fabric draped the forms of ladies and gents alike.

Homes of the upper classes were decorated with hand painted wall coverings produced by artisans from the Far East. Intricate patterns created unusual color combinations and colorful murals became a new form of art for the home.

Woven and batik printed fabrics used for upholstery displayed brighter, deeper colors and previously unseen combinations. Westerners accustomed to traditionally plain and colorless interior spaces embraced these imports. Even today, colorful textiles are still produced primarily in the East.

During the French Renaissance era, purposeful planning of these new, colorful options brought into vogue the first interior decorators, Percier and Fontaine. The realm of color, it was thought, was best left up to the professionals. We have these early color specialists to thank for the marvelously decorated interiors as preserved in palaces and villas throughout Europe.

COLOR, ONCE RARE AND SPECIAL, HAS BECOME THE NOISE OF THE EYES.

With the increased availability of colorful textiles, the use of color as an enhancement on the body and in the home had begun. Color production through the ages became simpler and more commonplace. Color became readily available and was used and appreciated by all levels of society. Having choices among multiple color options was normal for clothing, paints, even cars. Our love affair with color had begun.

As we fast-forward to today, the commonness of color has become like so much noise around us. The traffic sounds, advertising messages, the ever-present music and television voices have become a soundtrack to life. Airports and post offices keep us informed by bombarding us with sound. We can clearly hear the musical selections vibrating from the car next to us. Gradually, as we become more accustomed to noise, we are desensitized to it. The more noise we endure, the less we actually hear it.

Just as our tolerance of everyday noise levels has increased, so has our tolerance and widespread acceptance of color. Color, once rare and special, has become the noise of the eyes. As our acuity to sound has evolved so we no longer consciously hear most of what's around us, our awareness of color has also evolved.

Can you remember when television images were shades of black and white? Before color was part of the message, just having a moving picture with sound attached was sufficient to keep us watching the screen. Color was not yet used in that medium as a way to get noticed. Like early Western civilization wearing bland clothing, we had not yet experienced the magic of color on the screen. It wasn't long before our view on the television screen mimicked the reality of life.

Today, in order to get our attention, often advertisers, both in television or in print, use intense or shocking color. Interestingly, some savvy marketers have reverted to the contrast of black and white images to convey their message. On television, in print mediums, and in movies, the absence of color gets our attention as being different from what we're used to seeing. Different, stops us in our tracks, and the desired effect is achieved.

For the same reason, there is a renewed popularity of black and white photography in the art world. Its simplicity focuses the eye on the artistry of the image and is not distracted with color. When the noise of color overloads the mind, the calmness created by the absence of color restores the balance.

For the most noticeable impact, yellow and red are used frequently in advertising promotions. Those colors are wired into our subconscious as signals of alarm or action. Traffic lights and vehicle signs, in these eye-catching colors, are warnings to pay attention. McDonalds uses the combination so effectively, it's hard not to stop your car when you notice their yellow and red signage. Like a subconscious emergency signal, it's worked for them over one billion times.

Brighter intensities of color have made themselves comfortable in our homes as well. Traditional color choices are a thing of the past. Gone are the days of traditional white appliances. Stainless steel and black outsell white refrigerators. Remember when cooking pans were all silver metal? For the second year in a row, cherry red is the top selling color for cookware.

Common objects, from cooking pots to toothbrushes, have become color saturated. Manufacturers have learned that color gets our attention, and color sells. Why else would there an orange colored washer and dryer on the market? Someone must be buying them.

HOW DO COLORS GAIN OUR UNQUESTIONING ACCEPTANCE?

WHY ARE THERE SO MANY CHOICES?

Color is first introduced to us through fashion. Just as exotic silks from the East captured the attention of our ancestors, trend-setting colors have their beginnings in European fashion houses. High fashion dictates an ever-changing color palette. Each season, designers create new colors and combinations for the fashion conscious to see and to be seen in. The designer's client, with sophisticated tastes, strives to avoid the commonplace. Designers comply with the demands of the marketplace with the rapidly changing color introductions first glimpsed on fashion's runways. The looks are sometimes controversial, the colors extraordinary, and unlikely as it seems when you first see them, these colors are destined to become part of your life.

Will the season's color tone be somber or psychedelic? Look on the fashion pages of magazines and newspapers for color cues. Most every color we commonly use today was born in fashion. The orange, the hot pink, even the mauve, that we all eventually embraced. We could never have imagined these once unusual or shocking colors as part of our everyday lives. What was once shocking to our eyes, we now wear to work, drive down the highway, cook dinner on, and use on our laundry appliances.

Ah, the power of color to captivate!

Just as in ancient times, when pigments were rare, color use that begins for a select few, evolves into color for the masses. As quoted by George Bernard Shaw,"Fashion is nothing but an induced epidemic."

Most color, before it is accepted for general consumption, must circulate in society for a while. Color that used to take two or three years to get from runway to driveway now speeds through the process in mere months. Thanks to the internet and live broadcasts from anywhere in the world, we are much more aware of cutting edge trends, and much more accepting of whatever we see.

One color that began its life cycle in the 1980's, was referred to as Three Percent Green. The curious title referred to the top three percent of the population with the highest wealth. This deep green color, the color of money, was the color, so the experts advised, this select, 3% group of people preferred.

WE ASSOCIATE CERTAIN COLORS WITH PARTICULAR PRODUCTS.

The likeness to money may have been secondary, but it was "the" sophisticated color of the time. Think of a library filled with volumes of fine literature with dark green bindings, complete with a deep green, leather wing back chair. You get the picture. When advertisers wanted to appeal to this demographic segment, they used Three Percent Green in the backgrounds or lettering of their messages. Subtle, yet effective.

Luxury carmakers introduced the dark green shade, reminiscent of British racing green, on exclusive vehicles. High-end appliances makers produced commercial sized ranges and refrigerators to match the Three Percent Green cabinets in the kitchens designed to satisfy the demand for this special color. All was well and green.

For a time, Three Percent Green remained the hallmark of the elite. Until, (gasp), the lowly coffeemaker became available in Three Percent Green. More and more consumer products followed the trend until even the ubiquitous minivan of middle class America was produced in

Three Percent Green. The color had evolved with wide reaching appeal and acceptance by the masses. By this time, the color was more appropriately referred to as Hunter Green. The three percent population had already redecorated in the next, yet emerging color.

A trendy color sometimes becomes universally accepted by the masses, but most color that is uniformly accepted is traditionally a color range, such as earth tones, or neutral colors. These colors remain in favor because they satisfy a lifestyle that looks for enduring color. People slow to change, or who prefer not to change their color environment, can perennially live with undemanding, neutral color. The whims of fashion have little sway with loyalists of the neural color palette.

Color, such as Three Percent Green, can define a segment of the population, or it can create an identity. We each have a personal affinity with certain colors, but nowhere is a color identity more apparent than with the brands of products we use. We associate certain colors with particular products because of the strong use of color in the branding of the merchandise.

Think about a gift from Tiffany's and you picture their signature Tiffany Blue box. Picture a Ferrari streaking across the countryside and you most certainly see Ferrari Red. Even something as ordinary as insulation for your home brings to mind a bright pink color. Yellow Cabs, Blue's Clues. You can't separate the color from the product.

If color has such immediate brand recognition, is it possible to own a color? Imagine stating with pride, "I am Aquamarine".

Companies whose products are defined by their color have debated ownership of color in the courts on many occasions. Though product identity is closely linked with a specific color, the courts have agreed that a color cannot be copyrighted. No one owns a color. However, a product's manufacturer can petition the courts to limit the use of the same or similar color by a competitor in the same industry. Touché, Pink Panther. The court has ruled, we will have only one pink home insulation.

Color sets fashion trends. Color identifies. Color can also revitalize a timeworn product look. A change of color has breathed new life into products that were being ignored in the marketplace or becoming passé.

During a time when the population was spending less time in the kitchen and eating more meals out than in, Kitchen-Aid re-popularized domesticity by adding a vibrant selection of colors to their traditional countertop mixer. Suddenly, the colorful appliance in pink, or pistachio, or mango was a "must have" product in kitchens across America. We still don't make cakes from scratch, but we have the mixer to do it.

Apple Computer continued their brand identity as an industry leader in innovation when they simply added color options to the cases of ordinarily greige computers. By offering their iPod in brilliant colors, the electronic convenience became a necessary fashion accessory for millions. Something so much a part of everyday life, why not use it as a means for the color expression of its user?

The Volkswagen Beetle could have gone the way of all popular car models whose drivers grew up. Instead, a Gecko Green Beetle signaled the return of the classic icon, complete with a dash mounted vase and yellow daisy. Ecology minded flower children immediately identified with the color and the automobile brand was reborn.

The cultural significance of color is undeniable. Our early color training left impressions on our subconscious mind that effect our color perceptions today. Red, we may have been told early in life, is only worn by a woman of questionable morals. A black hat always identifies the bad guy. If you have red hair, you can't wear purple. Color rules were easy to learn and mandated to follow.

Wide acceptance of a color shifts our perception of it. The meaning of red has evolved from the sign of a hussy to the "Lady in Red", a very desirable way to look. Perhaps Nancy Reagan, when she wore red as her signature color, was responsible for making red a respectable color.

About the same time when cowboy westerns had ridden into the sunset, black hats, and other black apparel became chic and acceptable to wear, even if you weren't a bad guy. All it takes is for someone to bend the rules, get enough people to follow, and color perceptions change. And with red hair, it seems anything goes. Same with purple hair.

A widely accepted company uses a color as its identity, like brown, and suddenly the name of the color is synonymous with the name of the company. "What can 'brown' do for you?" Unassuming, nondescript, brown, the color of an old pair of shoes is now the identity of a huge company. In defense of brown, it is perceived as a warm, comforting, dependable color, just the image the company wants to convey.

> YOUR PERSONALITY IS REVEALED BY THE COLOR OF YOUR CAR.

Classic colors are colors that never go away. Fashion always changes, trends come and go, but some colors will always be part of our color-filled world. Remember your first box of Crayola crayons? The original colors of crayons, introduced by Binney & Smith in 1903, were black, brown, red, blue, orange, green, violet and yellow. These very familiar, rainbow-like colors remain classics. Variations of these hues, a lighter pastel, or a greener blue, debut on the crayon scene every year. Other colors, out of fashion, are retired. But the classic Crayola colors will always be in the box.

Color identity is also closely linked to who we are in the cars we drive. America, since the days of the model T, has had a love affair with the automobile. It is one more tangible way of demonstrating to the world how you perceive yourself, or perhaps who you aspire to be. Your personality is revealed by the color of your car.

Are you cool, calm and right on trend? Chances are you drive a silver colored car. That's the look car companies want to project with this popular color. Silver portrays an image of being in control, on the cutting edge and stylish. It's a neutral, non-color that doesn't take a commitment by its owner. It's not flashy or overtly trendy, an enduring color. But beware, the increasingly broad appeal of this color, as with every "hot" color, signals its inevitable demise.

Black cars can be sinister or intriguing, like a black limousine. The personality of drivers who prefer black cars tends to be aggressive. Self sufficient, Lone Ranger types are drawn to black vehicles. Of all car colors, black is the most likely to be involved in an accident. Perhaps because the dark color is harder to see, you reason. Or perhaps the temperament of the driver is has something to do with that statistic.

Conversely, the driver of a cream-colored car is controlled, conservative and self-contained. This color car is the least likely to be involved in an accident. Cream is just more visible, right? There seems to be a pattern here.

Change the color just a bit to white, and the driver of this car is a status-seeking extrovert. Again, a limousine comes to mind. Pearlescent finishes on white are the exclamation point of this personality type.

A gray car is comfortable to a sober, calm, dedicated person. Flashiness not allowed here. More understated than silver, more practical than black, pick a gray car to disappear.

If your car selection is blue, you're apt to be introspective and cautious. Like the tranquil images of sky and water, cruising in blue is for those reflective souls not susceptible to road rage.

A red car, on the other hand, means, "Get out of my way". Full of energy, zest and ambition, this driver moves and acts quickly. They may not know where they're going, but they are getting there fast.

Yellow vehicles signal a driver who is young at heart, idealistic and novelty loving. Not as many of these on the road. The yellow trend in vehicles resurfaces every few years, about as often as the resurgence of idealism does in their owners.

Green in nature is calm and serene, but in car selection, green car owners may have hysterical tendencies. Maybe because the color green on a mechanically based vehicle is so far removed from the color's occurrence in nature. Does this disparity bring on hysteria? Even in stock car racing, green cars are seldom used because they are thought to be bad luck. Don't ever tailgate a green car driver.

DON'T EVER TAILGATE A GREEN CAR DRIVER.

What about cars in pink or purple hues? Their occupants are likely to be gentle, loving and affectionate. They are true to their own likes and willing to stand apart from the crowd.

As a car salesman once told me, if you're concerned about resale, don't buy a purple car. No matter, I can't think of a lovelier color vehicle than Amethyst Pearl. It's what I have my sites on.

CHAPTER FIVE
Who Decides Color?

*H*ave you ever wondered why cars are made in silver, or blue, or red, or black?

Why do you see the color pink on everything from fabrics to phones one year, and by next year, pink is totally gone?

Where do colors come from?
Where do colors go?
Who thinks up those descriptive color names?
Who decides the colors that populate our world?

Color trends change with the seasons. Just as nature's color pallet changes as the months go by, the colors that are introduced in the marketplace change just as quickly. The difference is that nature is predictable in her yearly array.

Colors selections, as they are mass marketed, come as a surprise to most of us. The choices we are presented with each season for our clothing, furnishings, electronics and cars mysteriously appear. We see them in the media, on store shelves, on the car lots, and we dutifully choose them. Some higher authority deemed that we wear, sit on, listen to and drive products in the new colors of the season.

As with every choice we make in our lives, choosing to become part of the masses as a follower of each new trend, yields us the lifestyle that defines the masses.

One of indecisiveness due to lack of self-identity.

A life of conformity rather than creativity.

You pick what you're told to because you can't decide what's best for you. An absence of a clear self-identity makes choices confusing, so it's easier to go along with the trend. That way you'll be accepted as just like everyone else. What begins as the easy choice, after time, creates your image to the world.

The choices you make, however subtle they appear at the time, accumulate and create the person you become.

DO YOU WANT TO BE SEEN AS THE PERFECT FOLLOWER, OR AS A PERSON SET APART FROM THE CROWD?

Unlike nature's lifecycle progression that creates new colors, manufactured color trends exist to drive continuous change in the fashion and décor industries. Few things remain color constant in our lives. There are classics, like a black leather Eames lounge chair. Or the uniform consistency of Carhartt brown work clothes.

But as humanity has evolved through history, we have come to expect, even demand, color choices. Just as we would no longer be satisfied with black and white television, having only one color choice for most any product is unheard of.

Internet shopping is a great exercise in color choice options. Scrolling through the pages of the season's new clothing, I come across something that catches my eye. The photo on the web site depicts the model wearing a black top. The style, the cut, the details are all perfect. I can see myself wearing this style top for many occasions. Next to the photo is the arrow for color choices.

"Oh, there are other colors available!" Immediately the "one in every color" idea occurs to me. When you find something, you really like, "if the shoe fits, buy it in every color."

Clicking on the arrow to see the other options, the only color choice listed is black. I always feel a twinge of frustration when only one color choice appears in the pull down menu. It's as if I've been cheated out of the option to make a different color choice. Skip the color choice arrow and tell me up front, only available in black.

How much better (and more fun) to sweep the cursor over the name of a color, like on the Lexus web site, and see the image of the car magically change color before your eyes? That's not only choice, but also entertainment. Possibilities begin as pictures in the mind. This is visualization made simple.

SO, WHERE DO THE CHOICES BEGIN?

A color is typically introduced first in apparel. High fashion wows us with an introductory glimpse as models sashay down the runway adorned with the newest color. Soon clothing manufactures have copied the look and have duplicated the color onto garments widely available at local stores and online shopping. The true test of the color's acceptance has begun.

Clothing is a safe and simple way to experiment with a new color. You can literally try on a color, and, for a very small investment, make it part of your color environment. If you grow tired of the color, or realize it's really not for you, it's relegated to the back of the closet or the donations pile. Something new will come out next season to temp you.

The product's manufacturers also gauge the success of a color in the marketplace first by its acceptance in apparel. If orange had not been embraced by the masses first in shirts and shoes, you would not have found it a few months later on washers and dryers.

COLOR HISTORY DOES REPEAT ITSELF.

After a color fits comfortably in our closets, next it debuts in home furnishings. Starting as decorative accents, pillows, vases, or dishes, we get used to living with small doses of a new color. Do you remember what colors you wore last season? You can find those colors now in wall décor and decorative accents.

By bringing a color into our homes with small appliances, kitchen accessories, and the laundry baskets, we get us used to having a new color around the house.

If these small doses of a color are widely accepted, look for the hue to cover larger spaces like carpeting on the floor, paint on the walls, and fabrics on furniture. We'll see it in the patterns of wallpapers and in area rugs. Decorator magazines will feature the new hue on their pages and television programs will use it on the sets of popular shows. Do-it-yourself programs will show you how to paint and decorate with the new color.

Once we commit to a color in this, more permanent, way, it tends to stay around in our homes until the surface wears out, or until we're pressured to redecorate by a seducing array of new colors. Do you know of any homes that still have avocado green and harvest gold in their kitchens? Thirty-five years is a very long life for a color. These retro colors are coming back into vogue, but with different color names. Color history does repeat itself.

The more we notice a color shown in magazines and displayed in stores, publicized by the media, and used by our friends, the more we are apt to bring it into our own color space. Before long, we feel as though the color has always been a part of our life. Don't get too comfortable, though. Color change is inevitable.

Color's time line begins at the introduction of a cutting edge color, and its popularity ends soon after there is a broad appeal and acceptance of the color. Remember, color trends exist to fuel demand in the marketplace. And demand is mandated by the endless progression of new colors.

WHO IS THE COLOR GURU THAT INVENTS COLOR?

It's comforting to know, the colors you see everyday, from cars, to clothing, appliances to toothbrushes, are not left to chance. Colors that are destined to surprise us as they appear on the scene next year, have already been carefully and secretly planned. Colors we will see for years to come are already in the imaginations of someone's color-filled mind.

At semi-annual meetings, color conscious professionals from around the world gather together to map out the colors we will see and use years from now. The Color Marketing Group is the premier international association for color design professionals. Founded in 1962 and based in Alexandria Virginia, the not-for-profit association includes 1,000 color designers as members. The mission of this elite group is to create color forecast information for the professionals who design, manufacture and market color to us.

The CMG predicts the colors that are scheduled to appear in the consumer marketplace within the next 12-18 months. Industries such as Recreation, Consumer Goods, and Home and Visual Communications, pay close attention to the group's forecast of the next thirty-three colors you and will want to buy.

ARE THEY MIND READERS?

HOW DO THEY KNOW WHAT COLORS WE WILL WANT IF WE OURSELVES ARE NOT YET AWARE?

Awareness on their part is the key. The inspirations for their forecasts come from many sources. Cultural influences, the art world, entertainment, socio-economic issues, lifestyle, awareness of every influence around us all provide the inspiration for this group of color observers.

One example of how color cues were observed and collected from a significant art and museum exhibit occurred several years ago. When the Western world first caught a glimpse of the King Tutankhamen touring exhibit, the Color Marketing Group had already predicted that the deep blues, teal and gold colors discovered in Tut's tomb would capture our attention. Their prediction of our excitement became the basis for those same hues appearing in our fashion and home décor. Egyptian inspired colors and themes were common in clothing, jewelry, art and architecture because of their astute observations and resulting color recommendations.

Technology makes us aware of events across the globe. The internet enables us to see and react to events as they unfold. Worldwide culture and ethnicity affects our color trends much more quickly today than when explorers returned months or years later laden with chests full of unusually colored fabrics.

The influences of the global village have brought us dynamic colors such as Marrakesh Red, and a new introduction this year to the red family, Rubino. Look for this raspberry hue to appear in your near future, courtesy of the predictions of the Color Marketing Group.

Social causes create color change. Renewed interest in ecology is bringing nature's colorations, browns, greens and blues, back into favor in the clothing we wear and the products we use. Aqueous, a combination of blue and green is a new color you'll see paired with browns.

The color experts detect the pulse of even minor influences in culture and accurately predict the colors that will emerge as a result. Even variations in the economy trigger color trends. An up tending economy tends to bring in brighter, optimistic colors. When indicators are down, the color palette tends toward safer, neutral colors. Whatever captures the attention of the world, will ultimately show up as translated into the colors around us.

Color Marketing Group members specify color that will be used for everything from cars to tissue boxes. They get inside our heads. The product manufacturers pay close attention to their specifications in order to prepare their products in colors that their customers will be looking for and will be eager to buy. Color must be decided months or years ahead so manufacturers can plan for product, space and materials introductions. Even in our "just in time" production models, the color component is planned far in advance.

As the CMG members agree, color is a powerful communications tool that is used to create and reinforce a product's image. The correct color enhances the function and salability of a product. The wrong color spells disaster.

THE WRONG COLOR SPELLS DISASTER.

How often have you stared at a shelf full of wine bottles in your local grocery or wine store, not knowing whether to pick a Cabernet or a Shiraz? Ultimately, you made your wine selection based not on the wine's vintage or its hearty bouquet. Chances are your choice was influenced by the color of the wine bottle's label.

With the addition of eye-catching color on the wine label, a little known winery turned their fortunes around. The Yellow Tail brand of wine owes its Cinderella rise in popularity to a marketing makeover and redesign of its label. An eye-catching punch of yellow against a black background caused the wine to be noticed in the competitive wine marketplace. Since the label redesign, the same wine now flies off the shelves, making this Casella wine brand the number one imported brand in America.

"Color Sells and the 'Right' Colors Sell Better!" The motto of the Color Marketing Group is exuberant in its contention that colors make a difference in the marketplace.

As consumers, we may see, though not consciously notice, new colors appearing through cultural influences. We go to the museum exhibit, or watch a European soccer tournament, not really noticing the color component of the art or the uniforms. However, as we observe, we develop a sub-conscious familiarity with the colors we have seen. The sub-conscious mind, the seat of our feelings, makes an emotional connection with the color.

Is it a positive or a negative feeling? Our acceptance of a color, when it finally appears in the marketplace, depends on the color's emotional significance to us as we experienced it in the original cultural context.

If you first glimpsed the color at an exciting museum exhibit, you couldn't get enough of the luscious teal hues when you saw them in the marketplace. The color had a positive appeal for you. But, if the wrong team won an important sporting event, you were disappointed, and had a negative impression of the waves of the team's color exploding onto the field as the victors. Next season, the offending color appears in the marketplace, and you ignore it.

What color have you never liked? Track it back to an early exposure to the color.

I remember a sickly green color painted on the clinic walls in my grade school building. That green color was frequently used in hospital setting to counteract the affect on the eyes of the red color of blood. The institutional green spread to clinic and school environments. It may have been a lovely color of green, but I remember always feeling sick whenever saw it. Therefore, to me, it is still sickly green and not a color I like.

There are colors that arrive on the scene. You don't love it, you don't dislike it. Not all colors resonate with your emotions. What a roller coaster ride if they did. If you don't have strong feelings about a color, then make a decision to use the color based on these questions.

Is it a color that is comfortable and livable?
Is it versatile enough to wear today and still enjoy next season?
Does the color have longevity, or is it trendy?
Are you willing to live with it until it wears out?

A color without emotion attached to it can be worn and used in your environment, but it does not represent who you are. It's not your color identity.

Are colors ever rejected in the marketplace? Consumers reject a color if it's perceived as too trendy, or not livable. A color may be visually hard to look at, as were some acid hues of the '80s. Technology is able to produce colors not found in nature: punky greens, yellows, reds and purples, and harsh blacks intending to offend. These colors were not widely embraced by consumers. If a color doesn't work with existing colors, it will be a hard sell to consumers.

Visualize your home decorated in neutral colors. You are comfortable with that homogonous environment, so when the latest brilliant red color is shown in the magazines, it does not get your attention. What if the new color is a rusty, brownish red?

When you look at that color, your sub-conscious mind sees the worn paint on your childhood sled. You remember the first snowfall of the season, when you rushed to the garage and took down your sled from the peg on the wall, its runners a rusty, brownish red from a summer unused. You rushed to the hillside, flopped belly down on your sled, and wooosh, you flew through the snow. Winter had finally arrived!

Inexplicably, as you flip through the magazine, you are drawn to **this** new color. You can't wait to add the rusty brownish red to your home's decor. Why? It's just one of the many new colors this season. It's not exactly a neutral color that you're used to. What made you notice it? What caused the attraction?

It's a color that makes you **feel good**. Stronger than your conscious awareness, your sub-conscious feelings always direct your actions. Off to the paint store you go. Your result is a new, feel good space in your home.

THE MORE PLACES YOU SEE A COLOR, THE MORE LIKELY IT'S ON THE WAY OUT.

In the marketplace, color affects the perceived quality of a product, both by the color's look and by the color name. Consider the difference in the color offerings between Lexus brand automobiles and another common brand. Sapphire and Chardonnay are more appealing color choices to a discerning car buyer than Screaming Yellow or Vista Blue. Brands that are appropriately speaking to their target market know the look and the language of color that appeals to their customers.

This explains why not every color suggested by the color experts is appropriate to every product. Manufacturers gage the suitability of a color for their product by the historical purchase patterns of their customers. When considering a color that is outside of their normal color range manufacturers first test market the color to a small segment of their customers. The existing image of a product, if successful, will determine if its customers will accept a new color.

If it's time for a new image, color is the medium to use for a noticeable makeover. A recent television commercial for a credit card company follows the meteoric social rise of a wallflower, blandly dressed women after she charges her way to a vibrantly colored wardrobe. It's a 30-second lesson in the transformational value of color.

You are creating the brand called YOU.

By knowing how color works and by controlling the applications of color, manufacturers continuously encourage us to move to new color choices. Colors are inter-industry related, and as such, one industry influences another. As you learned earlier, fashion designers often start a trend when color is introduced in apparel. Because of the frequent changes seen in apparel, the styles, the hemline lengths, and width of lapels, the life of a color in clothing can be short. This is an advantage to us as consumers. We sample a new color in a smaller way. We try it on before committing to a relationship with it.

A color's lifetime, from cutting edge introduction, to easy accessibility in the marketplace, to over saturation, depends on how widely accepted it is. Color used to take six months or more to travel from fashion runway to shelves in discount stores. Today, the journey occurs in six weeks or less.

Communication technology gives us instantaneous news about color. The information is published and distributed worldwide. Production of colored goods is pushed into the marketplace. Clones of designer dresses are on the racks hours after celebrities at gala events wear them.

It has become a fast and furious pace for color. The more places you see a color, the more likely it's on the way out.

What about our vehicle colors? We may, though seldom do, change vehicles with the seasons. Cars typically outlast a shirt or pair of shoes. Even when you trade it in, a vehicle's durability guarantees someone will be driving it for years to come. But, even car colors are susceptible to trends. Evidence assorted teal colored vehicles still on the roads.

You may be tempted to paint the kitchen wall a fiery red, but your color exuberance may not follow you onto the road. Your vehicle color choice is a public advertisement of a personal preference. Vehicle manufactures have correctly determined that not all rainbow hues are accepted by their buying public. The occasional neon orange or bright green vehicle introduction just doesn't have the staying power of the more popular silver, red, or black choices.

Each model year offers the introduction of new color choices, but traditionally accepted colors have a longer life in vehicles than most other consumer products. Because we keep cars around longer, and they are a significant investment, we tend to select a vehicle color that resonates with how we see ourselves.

The experts predict the colors. The product manufacturers listen and create a colorful array for our choosing. When the experts predict a color they call "meadow green" will catch our fancy, how green is their meadow? Exactly what does meadow green look like to the manufacturers who will duplicate the color?

HOW IS COLOR COMMUNICATED?

There is a special language color uses to communicate assuring everyone's meadow green, or barn red, or parfait pink is a consistent color. The undisputed keeper of the colors is called PANTONE®. The self described, world-renowned authority of color, PANTONE® logs every color by name and a unique number.

I always thought, what an ideal job it would be to think up the names of every new color. According to Leatrice Eiseman, executive director of the Pantone Institute, the challenge can be daunting. Having identified and named thousands of colors, she draws on color associations, what a color looks like or reminds her of, such as Desert Dust or Soothing Sea. History and geography were her inspirations for Chinese Yellow and Coastal Fjord. Vegetation, foods, animals and birds are all sources she uses for color monikers.

"The fertile imagination of the colorist to depict a mood, paint a picture and most of all - to entice", indicates the enjoyment Eiseman's work with color produces.

The PANTONE® MATCHING SYSTEM is the source book of standardized colors. Much like paint chips or fabric swatches are used to aid our selection of color products for the home, PANTONE® has created color systems for graphic arts, digital technology, apparel, and interior design products. They provide leading technology for the selection and accurate communication of color across a variety of industries from designer to manufacturer to retailer to customer.

As the worldwide standard language for color communication, you have at your fingertips, a resource to experience every color. The ultimate effectiveness, the power, the impact of color, depends on how you choose to use it.

CHAPTER SIX
Any Color as Long as It's Black

*H*enry Ford is famous for saying it first. He popularized the notion of the superiority of black by his well-known, color-dictating quote.

"Any customer can have a car painted any colour that he wants so long as it is black."

His "one color fits all" approach may have had more to do with production efficiency than color trending, but our modern culture has accepted the slogan to define the perfect color as the color black. Associated with sophistication and elegance, black appears to be everywhere, yet the color black has the effect of magically disappearing into the background.

What's not to love about black? It's the dramatic color of an elegant grand piano, of a sleek stretch limousine, and a classic leather lounge chair. Black in our interior surroundings is perceived as the height of luxury. Gleaming black marble surfaces reflect the finest quality. Black velvet dramatically showcases the gold and silver highlights of fine jewelry. Black pearls are coveted as rare and exotic.

No wonder black has become the always-appropriate color, the tres chic, uniform of the day for the artistic crowd and the fashionably dressed. What else does the color black portray?

Black is a statement of non-color.
It is never trendy or flashy.
It is understated, aloof, and serious.
It is the ultimate "cool".

Think Marlon Brando looking fabulous in his black leather jacket, or Coco Chanel's striking silhouette in her classic, slim, black suit. It's an appealing look we aspire to create for ourselves. An image, controlled, serene, on top of our game. No one questions the man or woman in black.

Worn on the streets of every metropolitan center around the world, black is the color staple of urban wardrobes. The New York look, defined as a uniform of exclusively black clothing, has spread to encompass both coasts and all major cities in between. Wearing black has the powerful implication of strength, dignity and formality.

Black can also project emptiness or blankness, like a stark city silhouette, it represents the uncluttered starkness of city life. In artistic themes, and theatrical backdrops, black is used to convey moodiness and darkness, even doom. Images of the black plague, associations with death and mourning, are acted out against black scenery. Despair and despondency are communicated on a canvas by using black.

Historically, the color black implied submission. The tradition of priests wearing black was to signify their submission to God. Some fashion experts explain the allure of a woman wearing a black dress because it implies submission to men. The definition of black as a sexy color is undisputed. It's the color of choice for filmy negligees, stilettos heels, and various clothing styles designed for allure.

The popular, contemporary artist, Todd White, creates images of women, fashionably clad in black, as sensual and acquiescent. Male figures are aloof and equally urbane in black clothing. His imaginative figures and portraits depict an amusing yet poignant snapshot of metropolitan life.

Today, the widely accepted connotation of wearing black, for women and men alike, does not imply vulnerability, but power. The "power suit" is unquestionably black, although due to the overwhelming use of the color for any occasion, black's power to command attention is diminished. The over saturation of our culture by the color black means it has less visual impact than it once did.

WHOSE IDEA WAS IT THAT EVERY SUITCASE SHOULD BE BLACK?

Think back to the days when black clothing or hats, as worn by villains, were meant to make the wearer seem evil or foreboding. Witches wore black, black cats avoided, and scary figures, like Dracula in black, frightened us. For Darth Vader, black was meant to be ominous and overpowering. Black was not a color for everyday use. In the wardrobe, it was reserved for times of mourning and somber occasions. Formal affairs called for a black tuxedo or dramatic black dress. A figure dressed in black used to be attention getting.

Our culture and tradition is full of the insinuations about the color black, yet today it is the most common color used for all types of clothing as well as many other consumer products. If you've ever looked for your black suitcase on the baggage carousel, you know how ubiquitous black can be. Whose idea was it that every suitcase should be black?

Black is often the first color to be introduced for a new product line. The first telephones were black, most electronic equipment is made in black, and, of course, the first cars manufactured were only available in black. In deference to Mr. Ford, black is now only the third most popular car color.

Those who select black cars are thought to have an aggressive personality or to be somewhat of an outsider or rebel. Black implies empowerment, someone not easily manipulated. Loyalists of black cars love elegance, and appreciate classics.

Looking in your own closet, you probably notice quite a bit of this non-color. The color black, for most people, is the default clothing color that goes with anything. The practical starting point for building a wardrobe, black pants, or a black skirt create a foundation for easily adding other colors. A black jacket can be casual or formal and is seen as appropriate any time of year, for any occasion. Why not add more black to your wardrobe?

There is a truth about black that you may not know.

Not everyone looks good in black.

I'll give you a minute to let that sink in. The truth is, the color black is not for everyone.

The offensiveness is not in the color itself. Black would not be so wildly popular if it was hard on the eyes. It's not the hue itself, or the shade, or the significance of the color.

You may have your own theory about what wearing black **does for you.** The popularity of black in fashion is, in large part, because black is supposed to make people appear thinner. I'm not disputing that claim. Dark colors visually recede, making objects look smaller. That's a great plus for wearing black to minimize some parts of the anatomy. That fact aside, there is also a minus to wearing black. The detriment of black lies in what the color black **does to you.**

THINK AGAIN ABOUT BRANDO AND CHANEL. WHY DID BLACK WORK FOR THEM?

The color black, because of its density, has minimal light reflection. All light is absorbed into it. It looks visually heavy. The black leather worked for Brando because his dark hair and eyes created a balance with the darkness of the jacket. Chanel's signature black coiffure and intense eyes, along with appropriate black shoes, completed her balanced ensemble.

The important elements for successfully wearing black are contrast and balance.

Wearing black calls attention to whatever else on your body is similar in color intensity. Dark hair, eyes, or a separate reoccurrence of black in the wardrobe, like dark shoe color, will be reinforced by wearing black.

The darkness of black creates a stark contrast with whatever on the body is lighter. Wearing black works best when a balance is created between the clothing and the other colorations of the body, hair color, eye color, and skin tone. If your skin tone and hair color are light, the heaviness of wearing black will visually weigh you down and detract from where you want the focus to be, your face.

Here's an example.

Christina is an artist, slim and tall with long blond hair, fair skin, and delicate features. Her clothing is a consistent uniform of black, which she occasionally combines with dark brown or olive green. She believes, through her color choices, she is portraying an appropriate image of herself, the artist, reserving color only for her art.

However, the drabness of her attire creates an overwhelming contrast that makes her pale skin looks lifeless. The visual heaviness of the dark colors she wears finds nothing in her natural features to create a balance. The delicate color of her hair and her skin tone are weighted down by too much darkness. Like dragging a ball and chain, her natural coloration is shackled by the weight of wearing too much black. There is plenty of contrast, but no balance.

Hers is a commonly seen look for women and men in our black obsessed world. The color black is worn as an identity that robs the natural skin tone of its color.

Christina says she feels comfortable in black. She doesn't like light or bright colors, and especially not patterned fabrics. Why do you suppose?

Her color memories include being dressed in pinks and prints by her mother as a child. She remembers feeling conspicuous and ill at ease. Perhaps her early artistic longings were encouraging her in another color direction. Now that Christina is an adult, she wants a totally different color identity. She's in control of her wardrobe, now. In reality, it's her memory of color and the feelings they provoked that are in control.

Mistakenly, she believes that if her clothing is dark and colorless, she will not stand out. She intends to be the background for the art that surrounds her. Instead, her look creates a darkness that contrasts so excessively with her skin tone that she is conspicuously pale.

After much convincing, Christina reluctantly agrees to experiment by adding some color to her wardrobe. She wears a steel blue turtleneck beneath a gray cardigan sweater with gray slacks. This departure from her usual attire is quite a stretch for her.

The first thing I notice about her is how bright and blue her eyes look. Her eyes had always appeared grey when she was dressed in black. The coloring of her face glows warmly. Even her personality seems uplifted. Her color identity changed from somber to striking by eliminating the heaviness of the color black that had overpowered her.

Christina will benefit from color and see the improvement it will make in her life when she lets go of the belief that she should not be seen in color. Indeed, color is the only way we see her clearly.

For the sake of conformity or fashion dictates, too much black is worn, by too many people. The look becomes a uniform of bleakness. Black, nothing but black, as though the wearers are not worthy of color. Deprivation of color is not a natural phenomenon, but an anomaly peculiar to the human species.

Being ill at ease with color, or fearing you'll make the wrong color choice, it's easy to default to black instead of a more attractive color option. Until you realize you could be sabotaging your own success.

YOUR FACE IS WHAT YOU WANT NOTICED.

SHOULD YOU AVOID BLACK?

Because black calls attention to similar color intensities around it, check the colors in your complexion. If you have dark circles under your eyes, they will be dramatically accentuated by wearing that black jacket, making you look tired, not healthful.

If your hair is light, your eyes blue, wearing an all black outfit will drain the color out of your face and gray the color of your eyes. The look is severe rather than sophisticated. The heaviness of the black will make your face and head appear small and insignificant. Your face is what you want noticed.

If your skin tone is dark, wearing all black provides minimal contrast and balance. Sameness in color tone does little to set you apart. Black needs to be balanced so it does not overpower your personality. Black is fine as a starter, but the addition of other color adds to your un-forget-ability.

Coco Chanel recommended that you look in the mirror before you leave the house and remove one accessory, as "simplicity is the keynote of all true elegance." When you look in the mirror, if you notice the color you're wearing is wearing you, then you're not selecting your best color.

If you wear black because it's easy and acceptable, it's time to learn some new choices. Rather than always opting for black, try charcoal gray. Especially if you are blond, wearing gray conveys the seriousness and drama of black, but will not look as severe. You'll stand out amid the crowd of unimaginative basic black wearers.

Navy blue, although dark, has enough color to draw out the blue of the eyes and the color in your face. It's a good basic color that blends easily with greens and lighter blues, hues that would be overpowered by black. Navy displays a richness and panache you won't get with black.

What if your wardrobe is already full of black? Maybe you really like black. How do you keep from being overpowered by its darkness? Make black work **for** you instead of against you. Add another color when you wear black, especially near your face.

COLOR CHOICE IS ALWAYS ABOUT BEING YOU, NOT LOOKING LIKE A CARBON COPY.

A black suit will always work for you if the color closest to your face, the color of your shirt or your tie, complements your skin tone. Simply add one of your "feel good" colors. Since black can be worn with virtually any other color, pick what looks best next to your skin tone to wear closest to your face. You'll enjoy whatever benefits you perceive that black provides, but you'll stand apart from your singularly colored contemporaries.

When wearing a black shirt or sweater next to your face, add a jacket in another color. A patterned tie or scarf that includes black with other colors creates an intentional looking color accent. It's a trick designers use to effortlessly draw the eye to the focal point- your face. The addition of color will bring the attention away from black's overpowering presence. You'll look serious, yet sensational.

What about the occasion calling for a black dress or a black tie event? Again, think about balance and contrast even for formal occasions. Balance your clothing and skin tone when wearing that little black dress by showing off areas of skin to create a balance with the darkness of the dress. Wear a shorter length and go sleeveless when the occasion calls for basic black. Add colorful jewelry, a scarf or shawl to give you an uplift of color and set you apart from the "black sea" around you. Color choice is always about being you, not looking like a carbon copy.

The black tux is a relatively new arrival on the fashion scene, becoming popular in the 1920's. Prior to that, formal wear for men was traditionally white. Gentleman, if a black tux is required, you may have to rely on a handkerchief square or your colorful personality to make you stand out from the crowd.

The color black is destined to continue its reign as the monarch of mediocrity for the masses. Black is here to stay. Go ahead and enjoy driving your shiny black car. Get comfortable in your black leather chair. Keep searching for your black suitcases. Now you know, it's OK not to wear black, not all the time, not everywhere or everyday.

Liberate yourself from the sameness that surrounds you and realize the successful results.

CHAPTER SEVEN
The Absence of Color

If you find it difficult to commit to color, isn't it always safe to go with white? Isn't white always right?

Even though white light actually contains all colors, in our everyday world of sight, when we see white, we perceive it as having no color. We call white, the absence of color.

Think back to a time when products now available in Technicolor hues, were only found in white. When I was growing up, bed sheets were always stark white. The neighborhood clotheslines anchored rows of billowing, sparkling white sheets every laundry day. Your sheets had to be as white as the family's next door, or what a scandal ensued!

Every uniform in the medical field was typically white. Even the early McDonalds carry-out restaurants were staffed with men in short sleeved white shirts and narrow white hats. The absence of color was a statement of cleanliness rather than a fashion statement.

Good housekeeping practices dictated expanses of gleaming white for appliances and sinks in the kitchens, as well as all white porcelain fixtures in the bath. Bleach was a household necessity to keep the whites white and battle the dreaded "ring around the collar". That sounds archaic today. White served its purpose to communicate cleanliness in those days.

We don't see white used in the same places now. Bed sheets are multi-hues and patterned. Doctors, nurses, all medical personnel are seen in colors and whimsical prints. Consumers seldom select household appliances and bathroom fixtures in white anymore. What's left for white to communicate today?

White still says timeless. It brings a sense of order to any environment. The White House, named as such in 1901 by Theodore Roosevelt, stands for tradition. White reminds us of cleanliness and new beginnings.

A blank white canvas.
Apartment white walls.
Empty space.
Monotonous.
Boring.

WITH SO MANY OTHER COLOR CHOICES AVAILABLE, WHY CHOOSE WHITE?

If you have ever visited a paint store to buy a can of white paint, you discovered the endless variations of simple white. Cool whites, warm whites, off whites. White is easily susceptible to the influences of other colors.

The myriad of white choices are created by the addition of a minimal amount of another color that changes the personality of white. By itself, the paint chip's color just looks white. Next to a "whiter" white, it may look greenish or pink. It's not so easy to just pick white for everything in a room.

White also changes in relation to the amount of light that surrounds it. Ceilings are often painted white for better light reflection in a room, since white colored surfaces reflect about 80% of the light. By painting the ceiling white, the color of the walls is reflected onto the ceiling making the ceiling appear to be the same color as the walls only brighter.

Gretchen Schauffler, the color creator for Devine Color, Inc., a paint company located in the Northwest, explains the color white this way. "When I came to Oregon, people were using white walls, but they looked depressing and gray. We have a lot of trees that cover all the light, so there is a high sense of depression. I needed to create a contrast with white and beautiful deeper colors so the white would appear whiter and not gray."

She explains that white becomes whiter when used in combination with other color. In an interior space, a neutral color palette will work best when there is color in the exterior to create a focal point, a visual interest. The colors you see outside the window help to define the neutral color inside.

Wearing white creates a similar circumstance. White, without additional color, is lifeless. It appears gray in dim light, or harshly bright in sunlight or indoor fluorescent lighting. Our eyes are constantly searching for something interesting. White that appears grayish is uninteresting, dingy, like unbleached white sheets. Too bright white color and we are compelled to look away or go snow blind.

A huge improvement in the healthcare field has been the elimination of the traditional white uniforms. Not only is the addition of color easier on the eyes in the brightly lit environment of hospitals and clinics, but color is vastly more flattering with skin tones. Seeing colors other than "institutional" white puts people at ease in a sometimes-stressful setting. Color block patterns outline toothy shapes on the smocks worn by the assistants in my dentist's office. The colorful pattern adds an uplifting dose of whimsy and creates a diversion from the dentist's drill. Each season they wear a new design to give clients variety and create the visual interest our eyes love to see.

"VISUAL INTEREST" IS A TERM OFTEN USED WHEN SPEAKING ABOUT ART AND DESIGN.

White was once considered the standard for cleanliness and lily-white purity. The current trend towards holistic health is centered on vibrancy and life. Vibrant health, we are beginning to accept, has as much to do with the wellbeing that begins with our minds, not just the body. Physical symptoms appear as the results of our habitual thoughts. Since what we see is directly linked to the mind, our environment sets the tone for our thoughts. The severity and starkness of white does not promote a healing environment.

White has a curious effect on people wearing it as well. Just as wearing black near your face can drain the color from your skin tone, the non-color of white, worn alone against the skin, calls attention to the degree of color in your face.

Your skin tone becomes the predominate color of this color composition. The deeper your skin tone, the more successful this combination will be because you are creating a contrast. The paler your skin tone, the less white will complement your face.

The eye is always searching for differences and contrast. Like a young, inquisitive child, our eyes look for visual stimuli, something interesting to notice. "Visual interest" is a term often used when speaking about art and design. That simply means, a place your eye is drawn to, a focal point. Whether it is the color of the walls in a room, the colors used in a piece of art, or the color worn on a human figure, if there is no reason for your eye to stop and focus, it keeps looking elsewhere.

If your personal color palette is colorless, you have missed your opportunity to be noticed.

Porcelain pale skin with only white clothing next to it, gives the eye nowhere to focus. The sameness of the color tones forces the eye to find some small difference or imperfection to notice, like the redness in the whites of the eyes. If that's the only color that stands out, that's what is noticed. Not a positive impression.

White accentuates texture and calls attention to unevenness in skin tone. Picture a fresh snowfall blanketing the landscape. Every contour creates a shadow. Each branch is stark against the colorless background. The same picture is created when you are wearing white. That's why a five o'clock shadow abhors a white shirt. Successfully wearing white, demands meticulous attention to grooming.

When Queen Victoria first wore a white wedding dress at her own nuptials in 1840, she began the trend of brides wearing white. That popular choice for weddings has continued ever since. Her color choice was thought appropriate as explained in the quote from Godey's Lady's Book of 1849, "Custom has decided, from the earliest ages, that white is the most fitting hue, whatever may be the material. It is an emblem of the purity and innocence of girlhood, and the unsullied heart she now yields to the chosen one."

Custom, however, is never the best reason to select color. Whatever your reason for donning white, your wedding day, or because you already own white clothing, realize that you have other, more flattering alternatives. Even brides have multiple color options and dresses festooned with colorful beads and flourishes.

Remember the dozens of "white" paint chips. White, by any other name, may suit you better. A creamy white color, or pale shell color, though still white in its impression, will be warmer and more natural looking against your skin tone.

Is there a wrong time of the year to wear white? Of course, the traditional rule is no white before Easter and after Labor Day. White rules have less to do with the calendar and more to do with geography. Warm weather locales are appropriate for white any time of the year as long as white is balanced. The faux pas occurs when the color white, commonly thought of as a non-color, is worn as "go with anything" white shoes. They don't.

Only wear white shoes when you are also wearing white clothing to balance them, such as white slacks, or shorts. The brightness of white shoes will focus attention on your feet if they are the only white you're wearing, and your feet will become your most prominent feature. White shoes with dark clothing will forever place you in the time warp 50's era of Pat Boone. White shoes were his trademark look, don't make them yours.

White clothing, when it is paired with other color makes the best impression. If you are sporting a glowing tan from your tropical vacation, wearing white creates an attractive contrast and your skin appears deeply bronzed. Actor, George Hamilton is memorable for the contrast of his perennially tanned skin and perfect white teeth. Skin tone provides the extra color to contrast and balance white.

A pale complexion requires the addition of color with white to wear it successfully. Wear the white shirt, but only with a colorful tie, scarf or jacket. Strongly colored jewelry of turquoise, carnelian or peridot against a background of white is an eye-catching way to add zip to the plainness of white.

If your skin is dark, be mindful of the visual contrast you create by wearing white. The stark contrast between dark and light colors produces excessive muscular activity in the eye. The constant adjustment required in the eye causes the eyes to fatigue. The same thing happens when you read white papers on a black or dark desk. The muscles of the eye grow tired when focused on a highly contrasting picture. To soften the strain on the eyes, instead of a true white, pair a light neutral color, such as cream to tone down the harshness. Wearing an off-white with black is also a better alternative if your skin tone is dark.

Save your high contrast outfits for times when you're not giving a long presentation at the front of the room. Your message may be lost when your audience feels the need to look away to rest their eyes. Conversely, when giving a short presentation, as a master of ceremony, or when chairing a meeting, high contrast is attention getting and maximizes your importance at the front of the room.

The ancient Yin & Yang symbol graphically illustrates the interplay of black and white. This symbol represents one natural energy enhances the other. The color black is most dynamic next to white, and the color white looks crispest next to black.

Black and white used in a checkered pattern or geometric print represents a classic look. Clothing designer, Chanel used solid white with black trim on her signature apparel and made the pairing the height of chic. It is a timeless combination that you will always find as you shop for clothing. White House | Black Market, a chain of clothing stores, features exclusively apparel in these two classics, proving the ongoing appeal of the absence of color.

A GOOD RULE OF THUMB IS TO WEAR 75% OF THE ONE COLOR, AND 25% OF THE OTHER.

To successfully wear the high contrast of white and black, pick one of the colors to dominate your outfit. A good rule of thumb is to wear 75% of the one color, and 25% of the other. It's a matter of proportion. A half and half combination is eye catching in a small way, such as in a blouse or scarf, but alternating black and white the entire length of the body yields a busy, "jail house stripe" look.

When the two contrasting colors are balanced to the eye, you are sure to make a positive, memorable impression on the minds of your audience.

Notice whenever there is a Presidential address. The white shirt is paired with a dark blue suit and red tie. It is attention getting (contrast), serious (dark blue), but not too stark (not black). There is an accent (red) near the face to keep our focus there. In the subconscious mind, we associate this red, white and blue color combination as representing the flag, which is also placed in close proximity.

White is an important element in this scenario. White helps to create impact, but a white suited president would not be taken as seriously. The importance of the office calls for the significance of contrast.

You create your own focal point.

If your skin tone is one of your best features, wearing white will work for you and focus attention on your skin tone. White, by its brightness, calls attention to itself and whatever else is next to it. The connotation of the crisp, white shirt as the epitome of professionalism is still the standard in many circles.

Pairing white with a deeper color that creates contrast will keep the white looking sharp. For visual interest and extra impact, accent the white with a color that complements your face, rather than a predictable black or navy combination.

The absence of color really exists only in total darkness. White, whose equivalent in light contains all colors, naturally works best in our visual world when surrounded by color.

WHY IS PAPER COMMONLY WHITE?

WHY IS THE BACKGROUND OF THE EYE WHITE? WHY ARE CLOUDS WHITE?

To give visual importance and impact to the color that appears with white.

The written word is serious and important on a page of white. Typed on pink, or yellow, it communicates the frivolity of a party invitation, or ideas in their formative stage, like notes on a yellow legal pad. When your ideas are fully formed, you get your point across against a white background.

The eyes have been described as the windows to the soul. Sincerity is what we look for in a person's eyes, and we equate the clearness of the eye as an indicator of the genuineness of the soul. To exaggerate the whiteness of the eye, makeup artists have long known that by adding blue eyeliner inside the lower eyelid it appears to whiten the whites of the eye.

As for the whiteness of clouds, Gilbert K. Chesterton says it best. "White is not a mere absence of color; it is a shining and affirmative thing, as fierce as red, as definite as black. God paints in many colors; but He never paints so gorgeously, I had almost said so gaudily, as when He paints in white."

Imagine the heavens in billows and caverns of white, angel's wings and ethereal mists above us. On the orb of earth, as long as we inhabit it, we are treated to the magnificence of color.

CHAPTER EIGHT
Totally Beige

*I*s it a guy thing? You may be inclined to think so. Many men have a problem with commitment...to color that is. Not too bright, not too dark, beige is just right. It's the perfect "blend in" color.

If you're a guy, or if you know one, what color is commonly found throughout most of your wardrobe?

My husband is rarely seen in anything but khaki pants. He says he's being practical- they always look clean. I think it's a habit, an addiction... to sameness. He never has to think about what color to put on. Sound familiar?

In reality, beige may have less to do with gender and everything to do with color commitment. Don't think you're off the hook, gals, if you see mostly neutral colors in your closet. Why is it so easy to pick beige?

BEIGE NEVER GOES OUT OF STYLE. IT'S A SAFE CHOICE.

Beige, and all its other names, tan, caramel, ecru, khaki, is the easy, default color when you don't want to think about color. As our color conscious shopper, Jennifer, justified to herself in my earlier example, this color will go with anything. Wear it with green or red or blue or black. It mixes easily with almost any hue.

Beige never goes out of style. It's a safe choice. Just as those other "safe" colors, black and white, never go out of style. When each season's new colors are introduced, there is always a variation of beige included. No need to get rid of last season's beiges, unlike trendy pinks, oranges or turquoises that may date your wardrobe or your living room. Beige works in every season.

The allure of neutral colors in recent history has been as they are marketed for hi-end products. Luxury automobiles are enormously popular in neutral shades like Lexus', Chardonnay, Golden Almond, and Savannah. Because of their subtly, neutrals create an understated appearance, that does not call attention to itself. Exquisite finishes, fine lines and the appropriate logo are sufficient to communicate high quality.

In clothing, the subtly of neutral color can also convey luxury. A cashmere suit comes to mind with a masterful cut and professional tailoring. The wearer looks subdued, tasteful, and discreet.

In interior design circles, a neutral, minimalist look is described, in the words of furniture designer and architect, Mies van der Rohe, as "Less is More". Less color is more appealing. Stone and wood finishes are left in their natural state. The interplay of light and shadow create subtle color variations without additional color embellishment. This timeless interior design could have been fashioned in the forties or created yesterday.

With all the color, beige has going for it, the practicality, and the versatility, what could possibly be wrong with wearing beige?

As you learned about the variations of white, other colors are subtly found in beige as well. Yellow, red and gray as they appear in beige change the color to honey, rose-beige and taupe. Just because you're wearing all neutrals, they may not necessarily "go together". Those undertones of other colors may not "go" with your coloring either.

The word, beige, is from the Old French *bege*, a fine woolen fabric left in its natural color. Nature uses variations of the color quite successfully on her sandy beaches, creek side pebbles, and sheep's woolen coats. The reason why this widely favored neutral works so well in nature is because of the way it contrasts with other colors. There's that word again, contrast.

The sandy beach creates a foil against the translucent blue water. Next to the light brown pebbles in the creek are deep gray stones as well. The natural color of the sheep's wool is highlighted as they graze against deep green vegetation.

As in nature, beige is enhanced when surrounded with color. Beige has an identity, a reason for being there when combined with other color. It's not just a safe choice. It becomes a purposeful choice to provide a backdrop for other colors.

If you dress in beige, and its variations, from head to toe, you may be safe, your beiges may even be coordinated, but you'll never to memorable. To blend in and disappear, be beige.

To set yourself apart, you need contrast.

Is it scary to forsake your comfortable neutrals? Start slowly to ease out of your totally beige routine by picking a deeper, neutral shade, like chocolate brown or charcoal gray, to pair with beige. You haven't committed to another color, only a variation of what you're used to wearing. The contrast of the light and dark colors will give you more definition. More notice.

Deep blue combined with beige is an easy direction to go. It's not flashy, works well for the beachscapes, why not for you? Or, think about a desert sunset for another great combination with beige. Deep pinks, reds and purples add warmth and punch to neutral beige. Look at all of nature's combinations with beiges for ways to accentuate your beige wardrobe.

One of my favorite neutral, yet polished color combinations is a white shirt with a beige suit. This look works well for men or women. Wearing white with beige adds more visual weight to the beige, so it becomes the predominant color. Rather than being colorless, beige takes on more importance.

If your hair is auburn, that's another advantage as the red highlights in your hair create a pleasant accent color. Dark hair color creates a contrast that needs to be balanced elsewhere on your body, like shoes in a color darker than your suit.

Your skin color, if too pale, may not carry off this minimal color combination. White and beige with skin tone to match will make you look as colorless as your outfit. That's when an accent color, something that matches your eye color, will add pizzazz to the neutral look, as well as accentuate your eyes.

Richly colored skin creates the perfect, natural contrast with beige. A more pleasing neutral silhouette than the visual heaviness of wearing black, dark skin tones are enhanced by this lighter neutral look. Forego the basic black and let your skin tone glow against honey-warm beige.

Another color selected as a "safe neutral color that goes with anything" is gray. This color can appear cool or warm depending if it has blue or brown undertones. A steel colored gray will weigh heavily on you without a complementary, warm color to lighten it. A color in the red or yellow family is the perfect complement as these colors are found opposite blue, the undertone of the steel gray, on the color wheel.

Conversely, a taupe gray, with brown undertones, works best with a cool accent color. Kelly Hoppin, an international interior designer, writes in her book, *Kelly Hoppin Style,* "Be not afraid of taupe, for it loves pure white and dark stained wood, but beware, it hates yellow." Instead, pair taupe with the green and blue, cool color groups.

Are your home surroundings equally as colorless as your wardrobe? The "safe" color choice that "goes with everything" has provided the rationale for countless selections of plain colored carpeting, colorless walls and furniture fabrics in unimaginative, neutral hues. Even the Federal Reserve Board calls their periodic overview of economic conditions the "Beige Book". A real page turner, no doubt.

You may be a design purest and truly believe that less is more. You may just be afraid of making a color mistake, so you err on the side of blandness. What if you pick a color, and then you don't like how it looks?

As with any successes in life, the road to color success is also peppered with mistakes. That's how we learn. If you've never made a mistake, you've never really experienced life's possibilities. You haven't experimented enough to know your own capabilities.

As Denis Waitley says, "There are no mistakes or failures, only lessons." It's only a mistake if you never learn from that lesson. A can of paint is a small price to pay to experiment with a more colorful life.

ARE YOU DRAWN TO A CERTAIN COLOR, BUT YOU NEVER USE IT IN YOUR HOME ENVIRONMENT?

Do you think it's too bright?

Too dark?

Too unlike you?

Here's a great way to get over that. Pick a wall, such as the one you see as you enter your house, and paint it the color you have shied away from. No need to experiment with the whole room, just start with one wall.

Every day, the minute you walk in the door, you are greeted by a color that pleases you. No matter what your day was like, that life enhancing color welcomes you, and all is well. It may be a color you remember of the terra cotta houses from a western vacation, or the bright yellow of the beach umbrellas you lazed below. The color you see, the first thing when you get home, takes you away to the pleasant sub-conscious memories you have of that color. A vacation for the senses, created by the color memories of your mind. You won't consciously think about why the color is pleasing every time you see it. You will instead **feel** it every time.

"Feelings are like a color chart that God has given us."

– Keith Miller

If that small dose of color has the desired affect, now you know you're ready to use more of it. If your results are less than desirable, then consider it a lesson, not a mistake. Try making the color a little lighter by mixing in a touch of white, or tone it down by adding the color's complement. The paint store can offer suggestions for you.

Or start over and try a different color that attracts you. One color down and a paint store full of color choices to go.

An accidental dose of color greeted me on my own garage doors. Our house was being repainted while my husband and I were out of town. Before leaving, I reviewed with the painter that I wanted the same tri-color scheme I had used before, off white house, deep red trim, and taupe grey on the doors.

Something was lost in that communication, a color. Arriving home, we pulled into the driveway and were greeted by deep red garage doors. "That's not what I wanted," was my reaction. Notifying the painter, he was apologetic and offered to return the next week to repaint the mistake.

The next day, as I turned into the driveway, I smiled. My reaction was totally different.

"I love the red doors! They're perfect!"

The color resonated with my sub-conscious. It felt like a welcoming hug as I returned home. I still smile when I see those doors. They didn't get repainted.

There is a cosmic plan and everything happens in life for a reason. As Mick Jagger explains it, "You can't always get what you want...you get what you need." What I needed was a dose of life affirming color in my life and I got it.

How about you?

Remember the concept of visual interest? Our eyes constantly look for pleasant stimulation whether we're noticing a person or a place. People are easily bored when surrounded by sameness.

Why else would we so often hear quoted poet, William Cowper?

"Variety's the very spice of life that gives it all its flavour."

Ginger, cardamom, turmeric, thyme and saffron, not only add flavor for the palate, but exciting color that adds to our visual enjoyment of food.

From The Lure and Lore of Spices, "If the appearance of spices were to reflect their real importance in the history of the world, the bottles of spices would be filled with bright glittery substances, diamonds, rubies, emeralds or gold would be appropriate. When you opened the bottle, a poof of vibrantly colored, mystically fragrant, magical smoke would slowly billow softly throughout the room....Spices enable you to enhance not just your food, but many more important intangible aspects of your life."

Spice for the eyes. How appropriate then to spice your wardrobe, your workspace and your home with color to enhance all aspects of your life.

Totally beige?
Easy to live with.
Maybe.
Uninspiring, to be sure.

You create your life. You select your environment.

As with all the choices you make in your life, never be satisfied with less than you deserve. You deserve to surround yourself with color that makes you look and feel your best.

You require the richness and vibrancy of color to create your success.

CHAPTER NINE
Color and Power

*G*eoffrey Bradfield, a celebrated Interior Designer of international acclaim, adopted as his motto a quote from Oscar Wilde.

"There is an art to living- that life itself is, in fact, the first, the greatest, of the arts."

In describing interior environments of his design, Bradfield explains that his work creates "a backdrop for our lifestyles, to enhance and illustrate the way we choose to live". The home interiors Bradfield successfully designs mirror his clients' lifestyle. When the spaces are a true reflection of their inhabitants, the art to living, that greatest of the arts, occurs naturally, comfortably.

As the creator of the "backdrop of your lifestyle", each day you choose the personal environment of your clothing, the vehicle you drive, your home surroundings, and your work environment. The artistic medium you work with to create your surroundings on the visual plain is color.

You need not be an artist in the sense of a painter or sculptor to create. A subtle creative process starts the moment you open your eyes and you realize your "you-ness". As you rub the sleep out of your eyes and leave the reverie of your dream, are you smiling as you greet your day? Or, as you catch a glimpse of yourself in the bathroom mirror, do you close your eyes to the person you see?

How you see yourself is the biggest determining factor in how you are perceived to others. Are you portraying the true reflection of who you are, or does your mirror reflect the image of an imposter?

IF YOU'RE LOOKING TO BOOST THE SUCCESS YOU FEEL, FIRST BE COMFORTABLE WITH YOURSELF.

Being aware that you control your personal environment is the first step in making the changes to guarantee your success. Succinctly put by speaker Paul Martinelli, *"Awareness is our power to change"*.

Maxwell Maltz, in his book "Psycho-Cybernetics", writes, *"all your actions, feelings, behavior, even your abilities, are always consistent with self image."* He goes on to explain, *"By understanding your self image and by learning to modify it and manage it to suit your purposes, you gain incredible confidence and power."*

In other words, your level of success in life stops at the level of comfort you have with yourself. Why cap your success because of uncertainties about your self-image?

If you're looking to boost the success you feel, **first be comfortable with yourself.**

Being comfortable with yourself is not the same as the feeling you have wearing your old blue jeans and oversized sweatshirt. Comfort with your self-image is deeper than clothing level, below skin level. It starts at mind level.

Start with being clear about who you are.
You are different from anyone else.
Begin with self-acceptance.
Celebrate your uniqueness.
Self-confidence means you have belief in yourself.

"The person we believe ourselves to be will always act in a manner consistent with our self-image".

– Brian Tracy

Being comfortable with your outer image means the knowledge that you look your best, and then putting it out of your mind.

Obsessing about looks- it's the biggest obsession in life today. Advertisements, on television, in magazines, bombard us with messages, encouraging us to worry about the texture of our hair, be concerned about the shade of our teeth, to question the presence of lines on our forehead.

By focusing on the insignificant physical differences we each have, we are being led to believe that looking different is not acceptable. The assumption is- you want to look like everyone else, don't you? The same smooth hair, identical gleaming teeth, and perfect, furrow-less brow.

I'm reminded of an old episode of the television series, The Twilight Zone. At some point in the future, all the earth's inhabitants must choose from a limited selection of predetermined looks, models of "perfect" faces and physiques. Everyone is re-sculpted to look like everyone else. The heroine in the episode chooses not to change her natural looks and to remain unique. Of course, she is ostracized. What was a "science fiction" story is not far from today's reality.

The Italian poet, Petrarch, noted in the twelfth century. *"Sameness is the mother of disgust, variety the cure."*

Although we are encouraged by the media to look the same, we have always been conditioned to notice differences in physical characteristics. As children, we loved to play dress-up, to don a black mustache and glasses, or a wig and oversized shoes. When we looked different, we suddenly became a different person.

As adults, we are no less influenced by differences. Who do you notice in a crowd at the airport, in the coffee shop or walking down the street? Someone clothed in the ubiquitous, all in black, look of the city? Do you notice the figure of an unkempt, casually dressed person drinking a latte? Did you even see the person that you passed on the street?

What you notice is the person who looks different. Your attention is always called to the striking or colorful ensemble of a self-assured individual.

The way our minds are programmed, an image **needs to** be different in order for it to get our attention. To get that image to stick in our mind, it must be memorable. Remember the childhood game of looking at two seemingly identical pictures? We had to find and circle the differences. One picture had a squirrel on the tree, the other didn't. We were learning about the concepts of same and different, and being trained to look for the differences. We still use those early lessons.

Larry Winget, an author, speaker and a master of individualism, recounts the smartest thing he ever said about business success, *"Discover your uniqueness and learn to exploit it in the service of others, and you are guaranteed success, happiness and prosperity."* That philosophy holds true for personal success, too. Larry explains the undisputable fact. *"No one can compete with your uniqueness."*

WHAT IS UNIQUE ABOUT YOU?

HOW CAN YOU CAPITALIZE ON YOUR UNIQUENESS TO BE MEMORABLE?

Color creates the backdrop to life. Color surrounds us in our environment. You wear color on your body everywhere you go. Color is what makes you stand out.

STILL NOT CONVINCED YOU WANT TO STAND OUT?

Here are two important reasons why you do:

You feel better about yourself when others notice you.

Being memorable elevates your position in the minds of others.

From the time we are infants, the need for acknowledgement is hard wired into our psyche. Experiments with monkey and human babies alike confirmed that if they do not receive attention at an early age, it has detrimental psychological effects throughout adult life. We are a social species that requires interaction and acceptance from others as a way to confirm our own identity.

How do you feel when someone offers a compliment about your outfit, or when you hear a positive comment after you've had your hair cut?

"Someone noticed! Halleluiah,
I'm not part of the furniture after all!"

Your response may not be that extreme, but emotionally, it feels good to be noticed. Try it on a co-worker and watch their eyes light up. Abraham Maslow's Hierarchy of Needs ranked Esteem near the top of the pyramid toward the highest goal of Self-actualization, or being your best self. Self-esteem is crucial for experiencing feelings of daily success.

The acceptance and help of others acts to reinforce our own feelings of self worth. All successful people credit the support and encouragement of others in the realization of their goals. Attracting positive attention gets you **noticed**.

WE THINK IN PICTURES, AND FOR MOST OF US, COLORFUL PICTURES.

Once you are noticed, that is, made **memorable** to another, your image remains in their mind. Without conscious effort, your positive image easily appears in their mind. By one of nature's most predictable laws, whatever is in the mind, and in the thoughts, takes on the greatest importance and naturally becomes a part of life. When you're memorable, your image takes on importance.

Remember Maxwell Maltz's description of how we "see" with our mind. Once an image is fixed in the mind, it becomes part of a non-stop movie of images we "see" over and over again as played on the screen of our mind. Through the repetition, this image rerun becomes etched in the memory.

If you are asked to think of a beautiful place, you do not have to search through your memory banks. Your favorite image of a beautiful place immediately comes to mind. You have seen it over and over, instantaneously, whenever you access that memory. We think in pictures, and for most of us, colorful pictures.

You wear a color that gets you favorably noticed. Your image makes an impression in the mind of another because color is what we remember.

Anything that remains in the mind is naturally given more importance. Because your image is taking up space in that mind, your image is given elevated importance in that mind.

Think about your decision this morning to wear your favorite blue jacket, the one that reflects in your eyes and makes them appear the color of a deep blue lagoon. The flattering color gets the attention of everyone you meet. You feel great knowing that you look your best.

Later in the day, the phone rings. It's an opportunity for an important sales contact. The potential client requested you, "the person in the blue jacket". They saw and remembered the blue. It looked great on you, and it's you they requested. That's being memorable in color.

What if you had decided to "blend in" today? Wear the beige sweater that matches everything else you're wearing. You look fine, maybe a little pale. Your day is going OK. You're staying under the radar.

At lunchtime, you have a chance encounter with someone you have long wanted to meet. You respect her position in the community and she could really help you with your career aspirations. Here's your opportunity.

You introduce yourself and confidently ask if she would take some time to speak with you next week. She takes your business card and suggests you call her office to set up an appointment. This could be the break you're looking for.

It could be, **only if she remembers you.**

In that brief exchange in the deli line, with hungry diners calling out their orders, the cash register coins jangling, and noisy background chatter, did your visual impression stand out amid the distractions? Were you memorable, or did you blend in and she easily tuned out?

WHY TAKE THAT CHANCE WITH YOUR SUCCESS? WHY DO YOU WANT TO BLEND IN?

If you're a spy, by blending in, you can take action without being obvious. But covert action aside, there is no successful reason to blend in. If you feel you must look like your peers to gain acceptance from your chosen social group, it's time to broaden your horizons.

Why follow the choices of masses, the army of the plain, the colorless, and the unimaginative? What lies ahead of you if you do?

The answer must be found in what writer, Lewis Grizzard, meant when stating his philosophy, "If you ain't the lead dog, the scenery never changes".

"Never is progress achieved by the masses. Creation ever remains the task of the individual," Glenn Clark wrote in a decades old edition of Atlantic Monthly.

No one else can be you.

From a marketing standpoint, people pay a premium for uniqueness in the marketplace. An original work of art is unduplicated, it is rare. As such, it has a much higher value than an image that has been reproduced many times and is found printed on posters and greeting cards. Artistry involves unpredictability, that's what makes it art.

You have the artist's hand in creating the masterpiece of you. Color is your artistic medium.

Senior consultant for WSL Strategic Retail, Shilpa Bharne Rosenberry, advises that retailers must make an emotional connection with consumers to reach them. She observes that "shoppers can't control much in the never-normal world, but they can control their home and hearth." That control involves color. The emotional component that makes the connection is color.

"Products are made in the factory, but brands are created in the mind."

– Walter Landor,
legendary branding and design pioneer.

You are your best product. Color has the power to create your uniqueness. Set yourself apart as your own premium brand. Paint colorfully the original work of art- You.

CHAPTER TEN
Your Best Color

"People are anxious to improve their circumstances but unwilling to improve themselves, they therefore remain bound."

– James Allen

Developing a feel for color is similar to learning to appreciate great music or exquisite art. It may be intimidating at first, but as you immerse yourself, and listen to your intuition, you will be amazed what color says to you.

ART, LIKE
COLOR, IS THE
DESCRIPTION OF
OUR DREAMS IN
VISUAL FORM.

Visit an art gallery or museum and you may notice a certain painting draws you closer. You stop before it and begin to stare at it unselfconsciously. The world around you becomes inconsequential. You see no one else, you hear no other sounds. Something about that image is speaking to you, awakening sub-conscious feelings. It may be the colors. It could be the composition. Something about that image has captured your undivided attention.

If you listen attentively to those feelings, and the piece of art is available for sale, you take the artwork out of the gallery and into your home where you enjoy it further. Happily, it speaks to you every day and you are uplifted by its life-affirming message. It may make you smile, or bring on a sigh. It may transport you to a place where all is well. A locale from a childhood memory, a place you aspire to go, or a seemingly random composition of shapes. Art, like color, is the description of our dreams in visual form.

If, instead of welcoming the pleasant sensations you feel when viewing the art, you push those feelings down deeper, look away, and move on, you may later find yourself haunted by remembrances of that image. You may be reminded, at some future time, of those feelings you did not allow yourself to experience.

On many occasions, I have met a person returning to the gallery in search of a piece of art, that haunting image that has stayed in their mind for months. Ready to succumb to its attraction, they find it no longer there. Chances are, the image spoke to someone else too. Someone else, who heard its message, enjoyed the feelings it brought and took it home.

As the words of Sidney J. Harris remind us, "Regret for the things we did can be tempered by time; it is regret for the things we did not do that is inconsolable."

The appreciation of art is intrinsically linked to the sub-conscious, just as our perception of color relies on the sub-conscious to give it meaning. If a color is lovely to behold, and it makes you feel wonderful, you can appreciate the positive power that color has for you.

"What makes color so provocative is its peculiar blend of qualities both simple and complex... The pleasure good color brings rarely fades." so observes writer, Terry Trucco, author of Color Details and Design.

Color is the language of emotion. We live by the conscious meanings and everyday uses of color, but color speaks more dramatically to our sub-conscious through feelings and memories- some vividly remembered, some throughout our lifetime, we cannot forget.

The color red, that I am so drawn to, lives in my memory as a young girl. I vividly remember a particular night at home, the night of New Year's Eve. My mother was in her bedroom getting dressed for the festive evening. She had bought a new party dress for the occasion that I hadn't yet seen. I smelled her cologne wafting down the hallway, into the living room and I knew she was almost ready.

My sister and I were excitedly enjoying the New Year's party hats and noisemakers and getting ready for our own celebration. This was the one night of the year we could stay up until after midnight watching Guy Lombardo and fancifully dressed, holiday revelers ring in the New Year on television.

Suddenly, the bedroom door flung open and I spun around to see.

The most beautiful red dress I could ever have imagined!

Standing at the end of the hallway, she was perfection in sleeveless chiffon. The lovely V-neck dress was gathered at the waist with a sparkling, rhinestone brooch. The flared skirt was layered with flaming red chiffon that swooshed as she walked toward us in silvery, high-heeled pumps. That's an image I will never forget- an image of perfect color.

That image captured by my eyes was etched onto the screen of my mind. It has played over and over in my mind. The emotional response it produced was wired into the neurons of my brain, and into every cell of my body. When emotion is added to the image, it becomes unforgettable. That's the captivating memory color creates.

As a result of that color experience- I am forever enamored by the color red.

Not just red dresses.
Red cars
Red books
Red shoes
Red in art
Red candy apples

Well, also red dresses. I identify with red. I feel good in red. I look good in red. Red keeps finding its way into my life- and my garage doors.

WHAT COLORS ARE YOU DRAWN TO?

What colors did you like as a child before convention taught you otherwise?

What color did you pull out first of a new box of crayons?

What color was your favorite blanket?

The wallpaper in your first bedroom?

The shade of the tranquil lake that was your swimming hole?

Your first car?

Whatever color produces a good feeling for you, is a color to include in your personal colorscape. It will enrich your self-image and boost your confidence to be surrounded with this comfortable color. You will see yourself as a person of success.

"Whatever we expect with confidence becomes our own self-fulfilling prophecy." Brian Tracy goes on to say, "We will always tend to fulfill our own expectation of ourselves."

Think of color as a tool you use everyday. Like your computer or your cell phone, you could get along without them, but their effective use as tools to get more done and with more ease, contributes to your daily success. Color works the same way.

COLOR IS THE BEST TOOL FOR THE JOB OF DESCRIBING YOUR SUCCESS.

Color's job is to reflect the best you. To get you noticed as the vibrant and unique person you are. You may be able to get that point across without the use of color; just as you could hand write your correspondence instead of using your computer. You could also use a courier for delivery of messages instead of a cell phone. But why?

Color is the best tool for the job of describing your success. See how these color conscious people have promoted their success with color.

Sharon is a petite woman with a halo of wavy white hair. Her pale skin is radiant in the soft pink sweater she wears. She has a great color sense. Sharon stays away from the heaviness of dark colors that distract from the lightness of her hair and complexion. She does love to wear black, but always balances it with a lighter color near her face.

Bob is tall with white hair and sparkling eyes. He looks his best in a monochromatic beige suit and white shirt. The look strikes a balance with his light complexion and hair and creates a larger than life persona, effective in his line of work as a speaker. A dark suit, over the entire length of his body, looks unbalanced and minimizes his head, not a good idea since his face and voice is where the focus should be.

Paul is not tall. To create a longer visual line, a dark suit works best for him balancing his dark hair and eyes. Contrast is what you notice; his light skin tone contrasts the dark fabric, and a punch of color, a red tie. That's a memorable image.

Lisa's dark hair and eyes make her choices of reds and vibrant blues work for her. She needs the brightness of color to balance and contrast with her features. Contrast is essential for a true appreciation of life- its depth and possibilities. Pastel colors would not suit her as well because the deeper the color, the deeper the visual significance.

Oprah's lovely burnished skin tone glows in creamy whites and coppery browns. Her best colors do not distract, they enhance with subtle contrast. For a show stopping look, the contrast and punch of red is the runaway winner for her.

Keith has curly gray hair and deeply tanned skin. He has two looks that suit him. His favorite colors, sunny yellow and ocean blue, he wears like a postcard from a tropical destination, with his blue eyes, the sparkling seashells in the surf. To create a dramatic contrast, wearing all black attire draws out the whiteness in his hair and smile.

Becky looks and feels her best in light but lively colors, like turquoise and coral. Her skin tone is light, but not pale. Her hair is highlighted, though not blond. Lively color and prints give her contrast without being overpowering and complement her easygoing personality.

Cindy's salt and pepper hair frames her face. Her dark eyes are warm and intense. She loves the versatility of wearing black and she's able to balance the color well with her dark features. Colorful accents are what set her apart. She's never seen without a unique necklace, a colorful scarf or an unusual handbag to complete her dramatic look.

Anthony has closely cropped dark hair. A hint of grey at the temples contrasts against his deep brown skin. His profession calls for wearing mostly black and a small white collar. His commanding voice belies his warm and congenial demeanor. Father Anthony looks his best when, off duty, he dresses in caramel beiges and steel grey blues.

Jeanne is enjoying Mother Nature's color makeover. She can now wear beautifully her favorite colors, the blues and purples that accentuate her delicate gray hair and paler skin tone. Like Monet's lily pond, watery silk scarves surround her neck and have become her trademark.

Diane is a petite and fiery brunette with pale skin and dark eyes. Her job calls for a corporate look, but black is too overpowering for her small frame and coloring. She mixes high intensity colors, red, bright blue and golden yellow when wearing black, or opts for navy blue paired with pink, light blue or green. She knows color is what makes her stand above the crowd.

> SHE KNOWS COLOR IS WHAT MAKES HER STAND ABOVE THE CROWD.

Color families or "seasons" are helpful to determine the nuances of color that are flattering to you. The undertones of your skin and hair color will help you to notice if an orange-red or a blue-red suits you better. As you become more comfortable with color, you'll find the subtle differences fascinating.

Look back at the notes you made about the colors you found in your closet.

Have you eliminated any of those colors?

What observations did you make in front of the mirror?

What colors made you smile?

When you wear colors that aren't you, and choose to live amid color that's not you, it's akin to the deceptions practiced by mediocre painters of old. Not appreciating the perfection of the original art, they repainted with amateurish daubing over original masterpieces. Later, during renovation of the art, when the old, cracking, surface paint was removed, the true beauty of the original work of art below was uncovered.

Why cover your originality and beauty with the mediocre daubing of conformity? Realize your uniqueness as an original masterpiece painted with your own Color of Success.

"Successful people are not any
smarter than anyone else...

They have simply learned to use
what they have effectively...

And so can you."

– Bob Proctor

THE LAST WORD

"Aude aliquid dignum"
"Dare something worthy"

– Dr. Joe Vitale

Are you curious how Jennifer, Jack and Marie have redefined their color success? Let's find out what color lessons they have learned.

Jennifer's closet is filled with beiges of every shade and nuance. She has sorted through the ones that made her look too pale, the ones that looked yellow, and the ones she never really liked. She keeps only the pieces that fit her well and are of the finest quality. She has a good foundation for her future wardrobe. The local Goodwill is happy to receive the donations of the other clothing.

She calls Pam at Chico's and invites her for lunch. "I could use your help, Pam," Jennifer begins. "I'm not sure which colors are best for me. Can you help?"

Over coffee, Pam makes her observations of the colors that have looked the best on Jennifer. Jennifer takes some notes as Pam suggests several colors that flatter her skin tone and hair color.

"Thanks, Pam. I'll be in at the end of the week."

Looking through the list of colors, Jennifer visualizes each one. As she does, she pays attention to her feelings about each color. Some colors she feels indifferent about. Others are not her favorites. She discovers a handful of colors that make her feel good. They bring a smile to her face as she traces back fond memories.

> IT'S THE BLUE OF THE SEA THAT BRINGS OUT THE COLOR OF HER EYES.

The pink of her first bicycle, and of the homemade icing on her birthday cake. It's the deep, velvety color of a June rose.

The bright blue of the sky on a summer day and of the bluebells that filled her neighborhood field. It's the blue of the sea that brings out the color of her eyes.

The mint green of the candies her grandmother rewarded her with after helping with the dishes. The green of mint juleps enjoyed with friends on Derby day.

She returns to Chico's with her list of favored colors. Pam brings Jennifer several pieces of clothing to try on in the colors she requested.

"You were right, Pam, this color looks great on me." And feels great, too, Jennifer nods at her pink reflection. The roses in her cheeks create a matching glow. "Shopping is so much easier when I know what I want."

Pam then brings out a new color that has just arrived. "This color would also look good on you, Jennifer." She holds the jacket in front of her reflection. The color of a ripe cantaloupe comes to mind.

"Hmmm. I do like it- but I don't love it. It would go well with my beige basics. Let me think about it." Jennifer's priority is to populate her closet with "love it" colors first.

Jennifer makes her purchases with the self-satisfaction than now, with the right colors on her side, she looks her best. And people will notice. She's got the feeling, the Color of Success.

Jack pulls away from the Lexus dealership behind the wheel of the Mercury Metallic SC430. He knows what he needs to do. After a spin around the block, he returns. Scott is still outside, with a quizzical look on his face.

"Now that I've had my test drive," Jack answers his questioning look, "I'm ready for my Obsidian Black model." Scott now realizes that Jack is a person that knows what he wants.

"Right!" Scott agrees. "You know, Jack, we just got one in. It hasn't even been prepped yet. Why don't you get some lunch. I'll have it ready for you in an hour. Go ahead and drive that car." Scott sends him off with a wave and hurries into the showroom.

"That sounds, great!" Jack speeds off to grab some lunch. "I'm going to need some new sunglasses to wear in my convertible." Jack stops at the Sunglass Shack and selects a wrap around pair with black frames. He tries them on and nods, "Perfect."

Back at the Lexus dealership, Scott has Jack's car waiting prominently out front. "Wow!" He exclaims as he pulls in. "This **is** my dream come true."

After swapping keys and updating the paperwork, Jack is on his way. He puts on his black shades and starts his car. Breathing deeply, he doesn't have to close his eyes this time. Jack is living his dream. He is the person he sees himself as being, surrounded with his Color of Success.

Marie pours another glass of wine for her friend, Nicole. "You know, Nicole, your sofa is almost as old as mine was. Maybe it's time for something new for you."

"Yes, looking at your beautiful sofa makes me want one, too," Nicole looks dreamily at Marie's new black leather sofa. "I really should."

"Nicole, since you like this sofa so well, why don't you buy this one from me and I'll get the other one I liked?" Marie's image of that fabulous, red leather sofa is etched in her mind.

"Really?" Nicole is all smiles. She's already seeing the luxurious black sofa in her own living room. "That red one would look fine in here, Marie, if you added a few red toss pillows in the chairs. I saw some the other day. Where was that?"

Marie is already picking up the phone and calling the furniture store. "Do you still have the red leather sofa I looked at yesterday?"

The salesman assures her they do, all the while he's wondering what she's up to.

"Would your delivery people move the black sofa to another address? It's only a few blocks away." Marie nods to Nicole his reply. "Great! That red sofa is mine!"

Marie breathes a sigh of satisfaction and thinks, "That color **is** so me."

"Nicole, where did you see those red pillows?"

Marie made the decision to listen to her true self and surround herself with the color that speaks to her, the Color of Success.

It's never too late to discover who you are.

And to give yourself permission to **be you.**

ENJOY YOU OWN COLOR OF SUCCESS!

"There is only one corner of the universe you can be certain of improving and this is your own self"

– Aldous Huxley

Visit www.thecolorofsuccessbook.com and click on
Contact Me for your FREE gift and monthly Color Tips
and Trends to keep you looking & feeling TERRIFIC!

Let me know about your Color Success
melapp@gaslightgallery.net

ABOUT THE AUTHOR

An expert Colorist, Mary Ellen Lapp has perfected her talents and entrepreneurial skills through her Interior Design Business, and Contemporary Art Galleries. She explains her lifelong observation and study of Color appropriately, "Color is my Life". Focusing on creating life enhancing Colorscapes for the interior spaces of clients, her expertise has transformed restaurant interiors, office environments, retail spaces and private homes.

In addition to physical spaces, Mary Ellen works with clients to create their own personal Color identity to attract positive outcomes in their lives. Mary Ellen Lapp is a Certified LifeSuccess Consultant and Coach...

Her interaction with clients explores the integral link between their self image and life results. Describing color's profound impact on success, personally, professionally, and emotionally, Mary Ellen writes on the influences of color, and presents LifeSuccess programs worldwide. LifeSuccess products and techniques help clients to BE more, DO more and HAVE more.

Mary Ellen divides her time between the tranquil beauty of Northern Michigan and the alluring Caribbean Islands with her husband, Keith.

RECOMMENDED RESOURCES

ELITE LEXUS OF LANSING

5575 S. Pennsylvania
Lansing, MI 48911
(800) 539-8748
Rosario Criscuolo – Owner
www.lexusoflansing.com

 GASLIGHT GALLERY

200 Howard St
Petoskey MI 49770
866-348-5079
www.gaslightgallery.net

CHICO'S

11215 Metro Parkway
Fort Meyers, FL 33966
(888) 855-4986
www.chicos.com

Simon Bull Studios

740 Redwood Avenue
Sand City, CA 93955
(831) 393-9131
www.bullart.com

MERLE NORMAN®

9130 Bellanca Avenue
Los Angeles, CA 90045
(800) 421-6648
www.merlenorman.com

GEOFFREY BRADFIELD, INC.

116 E. 61st Street
New York, NY 10021
(212) 758-1773
www.geoffreybradfield.com

Devine Color

Gretchen Schauffler
12006 SW Garden Place
Portland, OR 97223
(866) 926-5677
www.devinecolor.com

Susan G. Komen
FOR THE CURE

5005 LBJ Freeway
Suite 250
Dallas, TX 75244
(972) 855-1600
www.komen.org

OTHER BOOKS FROM LifeSuccess Publishing

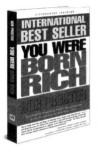

You Were Born Rich

Bob Proctor
ISBN # 978-0-9656264-1-5

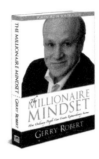

The Millionaire Mindset
*How Ordinary People Can
Create Extraordinary Income*

Gerry Robert
ISBN # 978-1-59930-030-6

Rekindle The Magic In
Your Relationship
Making Love Work

Anita Jackson
ISBN # 978-1-59930-041-2

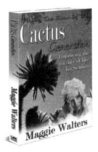

Finding The Bloom of
The Cactus Generation
*Improving the quality of
life for Seniors*

Maggie Walters
ISBN # 978-1-59930-011-5

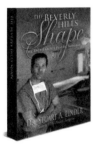

The Beverly Hills Shape
The Truth About Plastic Surgery

Dr. Stuart Linder
ISBN # 978-1-59930-049-8

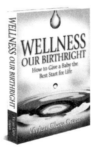

Wellness Our Birthright
*How to give a baby the best
start in life.*

Vivien Clere Green
ISBN # 978-1-59930-020-7

Lighten Your Load

Peter Field
ISBN # 978-1-59930-000-9

Change & How To
Survive In The New
Economy
*7 steps to finding freedom
& escaping the rat race*

Barrie Day
ISBN # 978-1-59930-015-3

OTHER BOOKS FROM LifeSuccess Publishing

Stop Singing The Blues
*10 Powerful Strategies For
Hitting The High Notes In
Your Life*

Dr. Cynthia Barnett
ISBN # 978-1-59930-022-1

Don't Be A Victim,
*Protect Yourself
Everything Seniors Need To
Know To Avoid Being Taken
Financially*

Jean Ann Dorrell
ISBN # 978-1-59930-024-5

A "Hand Up", not a
"Hand Out"
*The best ways to help others
help themselves*

David Butler
ISBN # 978-1-59930-071-9

Doctor Your Medicine Is
Killing Me!
*One Mans Journey From
Near Death to Health and
Wellness*

Pete Coussa
ISBN # 978-1-59930-047-4

I Believe in Me
*7 Ways for Woman to Step
Ahead in Confidence*

Lisa Gorman
ISBN # 978-1-59930-069-6

The Color of Success
*Why Color Matters in your
Life, your Love, your Lexus*

Mary Ellen Lapp
ISBN # 978-1-59930-078-8

If Not Now, When?
What's Your Dream?

Cindy Nielsen
ISBN # 978-1-59930-073-3

The Skills to Pay the
Bills… and then some!
*How to inspire everyone in
your organisation into high
performance!*

Buki Mosaku
ISBN # 978-1-59930-058-0

The Secret To Cracking
The Property Code
7 Timeless Principles for
Successful Real Estate
Investment

Richard S.G. Poole
ISBN # 978-1-59930-063-4

Why My Mother Didn't
Want Me To Be Psychic
The Intelligent Guide To The
Sixth Sense

Heidi Sawyer
ISBN # 978-1-59930-052-8

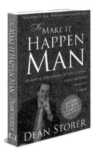

The Make It Happen Man
10 ways to turn obstacles
into stepping stones without
breaking a sweat

Dean Storer
ISBN # 978-1-59930-077-1

Change your body
Change your life
with the Fittest Couple in
the World

Matt Thom &
Monica Wright
ISBN # 978-1-59930-065-8

Good Vibrations!
Can you tune in to a more
positive life?

Clare Tonkin
ISBN # 978-1-59930-064-1

The Millionaire Genius
How to wake up the money
magic within you.

David Ogunnaike
ISBN # 978-1-59930-026-9

Scoring Eagles
Improve Your Score In Golf,
Business and Life

Max Carbone
ISBN # 978-1-59930-045-0

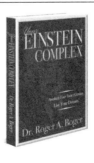

The Einstein Complex
Awaken your inner genius,
live your dream.

Dr. Roger A. Boger
ISBN # 978-1-59930-055-9

OTHER BOOKS FROM LIFESUCCESS PUBLISHING

Break Through to You
How to Change Your World Through the Power of You!

Lisa Watson
ISBN # 978-1-59930-084-9

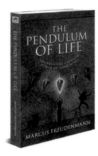

The Pendulum of Life
Unleash the Creative Power of Your Mind

Marcus Freudenmann
ISBN # 978-1-59930-075-7

The Sweet Smell of Success
Health & Wealth Secrets

James "Tad" Geiger M.D.
ISBN # 978-1-59930-088-7

Living the Law of Attraction
Real Stories of People Manifesting Wealth, Health and Happiness

Rich German, Andy Wong & Robin Hoch
ISBN # 978-1-59930-091-7

Wealth Matters
Abundance is Your Birthlight

Chris J. Snook with Chet Snook
ISBN # 978-1-59930-096-2

The Success Toolbox
For Entrepreneurs

Janis Vos
ISBN # 978-1-59930-005-4

Chemical Free Kids
Raising Healthy Children in a Toxic World

Dr. Sarah Lantz
ISBN # 978-1-59930-072-6

The Girlz Guide to Building Wealth
...and men like it too

Maya Galletta, Aaron Cohen, Polly McCormick, Mike McCormick
ISBN # 978-1-59930-048-1